Getting Started with NativeScript

Explore the possibility of building truly native, cross-platform mobile applications using your JavaScript skill—NativeScript!

Nathanael J. Anderson

BIRMINGHAM - MUMBAI

Getting Started with NativeScript

First published: January 2016

Production reference: 1220116

Published by Packt Publishing Ltd.
Livery Place
35 Livery Street
Birmingham B3 2PB, UK.

ISBN 978-1-78588-865-6

www.packtpub.com

Credits

Author
Nathanael J. Anderson

Reviewer
TJ VanToll

Commissioning Editor
Veena Pagare

Acquisition Editor
Prachi Bisht

Content Development Editor
Mehvash Fatima

Technical Editor
Abhishek R. Kotian

Copy Editor
Lauren Harkins

Project Coordinator
Shipra Chawhan

Proofreader
Safis Editing

Indexer
Monica Ajmera Mehta

Production Coordinator
Conidon Miranda

Cover Work
Conidon Miranda

Foreword

Are you tired of writing the same mobile app from scratch for iOS, Android and Windows? Yes? Then, you should be glad you found NativeScript!

Owing to the mobile platforms diversification, it is clear that to build a successful mobile application, you should make it available on all of the major mobile marketplaces, namely, Apple AppStore, Google PlayStore, and Microsoft Windows Store. This created a need for companies and developers to publish native apps that are available on all three major mobile stores without compromising on the native user experience. The problem, however, is that these three operating systems are very different and companies need to implement three different applications for these stores. Essentially, your company has to write and maintain multiple implementations for the same problem. Teams write (and have to support) the same apps multiple times. There is a good chance that bugs reported on one platform also exist on the others but remain unnoticed. Apps that are meant to behave identically on all platforms may exhibit subtle differences due to their differing implementations. Also, shipping new features at the same time on all platforms is difficult. This is neither optimal, nor very productive and requires a significant investment to gain the knowledge of three different operating systems, languages, IDEs, APIs, and marketplaces. There has got to be a better way. Enter NativeScript—a framework using the native platform APIs, rendering and layout capabilities to deliver ultimate user experience and will allow developers to reuse their coding skills, eliminating the need to learn new languages and IDEs.

The NativeScript framework enables developers to use the pure JavaScript language to build native mobile applications running on all major mobile platforms—Apple iOS, Google Android, and Windows Universal. The application's UI stack is built on the native platform rendering and layout engine using native UI components, and because of that, no compromises with the User Experience of the applications are made. It is also worth mentioning that a full native API access is provided using JavaScript.

This book has everything you need to get started with NativeScript. It starts with the fundamentals, such as the project structure, the command-line interface, how to use basic UI element, how to use third-party native components, and finally, how to target different platforms with NativeScript.

The author, Nathanael Anderson, is one of the faces of NativeScript. He has a deep understanding of how the framework operates from inside out and is the best person who can teach you how to use it.

> *"I'm confident that by reading this book, you will be able to quickly get into NativeScript and start building your next cross-platform native mobile application."*

Valio Stoychev

Product Manager NativeScript at Telerik

About the Author

Nathanael J. Anderson has been developing software for over 20 years in a wide range of industries, including areas of games, time management, imaging, service, printing, accounting, land management, security, web, and even (believe it or not) some successful government projects. He is currently a contract developer for master technology and can create a solution for several types of applications (native, web, mobile, and hybrid) running on any operating system.

As a senior developer engineer, he can work, tune, and secure everything from your backend servers to the final destination of the data on your desktop or mobile devices. By understanding the entire infrastructure, including the real and virtualized hardware, he can completely eliminate different types of issues in all parts of a framework.

Currently, he has multiple highly rated cross-platform plugins for NativeScript, and he works heavily in the NativeScript community by providing things such as bleeding edge build servers to build knightly code. He has also provided multiple patches and features to the main NativeScript project.

About the Reviewer

TJ VanToll is a senior developer advocate for Telerik, a jQuery team member, and the author of *jQuery UI in Action*. He has over a decade of web development experience—specializing in performance and the mobile Web. He speaks about his research and experiences at conferences around the world and has written for publications such as Smashing Magazine, HTML5 Rocks, and MSDN Magazine. You can follow him on Twitter at `@tjvantoll` and on GitHub at `tjvantoll`.

www.PacktPub.com

Support files, eBooks, discount offers, and more

For support files and downloads related to your book, please visit `www.PacktPub.com`.

Did you know that Packt offers eBook versions of every book published, with PDF and ePub files available? You can upgrade to the eBook version at `www.PacktPub.com` and as a print book customer, you are entitled to a discount on the eBook copy. Get in touch with us at `service@packtpub.com` for more details.

At `www.PacktPub.com`, you can also read a collection of free technical articles, sign up for a range of free newsletters and receive exclusive discounts and offers on Packt books and eBooks.

`https://www2.packtpub.com/books/subscription/packtlib`

Do you need instant solutions to your IT questions? PacktLib is Packt's online digital book library. Here, you can search, access, and read Packt's entire library of books.

Why subscribe?

- Fully searchable across every book published by Packt
- Copy and paste, print, and bookmark content
- On demand and accessible via a web browser

Free access for Packt account holders

If you have an account with Packt at `www.PacktPub.com`, you can use this to access PacktLib today and view 9 entirely free books. Simply use your login credentials for immediate access.

Table of Contents

Preface

Welcome to *Getting Started with NativeScript*. In this book, we are going to go on an awesome journey of building cross-platform applications in JavaScript. We will cover everything from how NativeScript works, to how to test, debug, and finally deploy your application. Over the course of this book, we are going to explore how to build a full-featured, cross-platform messaging platform. The application will work the same on all NativeScript-supported platforms. With your ability to develop in JavaScript and the insights provided in this book, you will be releasing your own cool applications in no time.

What this book covers

Chapter 1, Introduction to NativeScript, will teach you about NativeScript and how to install and build your first NativeScript application.

Chapter 2, The Project Structure, provides an overview of what all the different files and folders are used for, and we will build and switch to a second screen for our application here.

Chapter 3, Declarative UI, Styling, and Events, works through how to create screens using the Declarative UI, style them and then how to create and respond to events.

Chapter 4, Building a Featured Application, helps you to actually sit down and build a full-featured, cross-device messaging application using just the standard NativeScript components.

Chapter 5, Installing Third-Party Components, delves into how to install several different types of third-party components to enhance our cool communication application.

Chapter 6, Platform Differences, looks at how to deal with the differences between iOS and Android and the differences in the actual physical characteristics of the devices even on the same platform.

Chapter 7, Testing and Deploying Your App, looks at how to use several different types of testing frameworks, how to debug your application, and finally, how to actually deploy your application.

What you need for this book

NativeScript is an open source project; as such, it uses technologies that can be freely downloaded from the Internet. You need to download and install a recent version of Node from `http://nodejs.org`. You also need a text editor so that you can edit your source code. If you are developing for Android, you need to download and install Java 7, Gradle 2.3, and the Android SDK. For iOS, you need to install Xcode 6.2 or a later version.

Who this book is for

If you are already a JavaScript developer and you want to finally build native cross-platform applications for iOS and Android using your skills, then this book is just for you!

Conventions

In this book, you will find a number of styles of text that distinguish between different kinds of information. Here are some examples of these styles, and an explanation of their meaning.

Code words in text are shown as follows: "which a `require` statement would load into your code."

A block of code is set as follows:

```
{
  "name": "tns-template-hello-world",
  "main": "app.js",
  "version": "1.5.0",
  ... more json documentation fields...
}
```

When we wish to draw your attention to a particular part of a code block, the relevant lines or items are set in bold:

```
{
  "nativescript": {
    "id": "org.nativescript.crossCommunicator",
    "tns-android": {
      "version": "1.5.0"
    },
```

Any command-line input is written as follows:

```
nativescript run ios --emulator
```

New terms and *important words* are shown in bold or italics. Words that you see on the screen, in menus or dialog boxes for example, appear in the text like this: "You can probably guess that the Label will still say **Tap the button**."

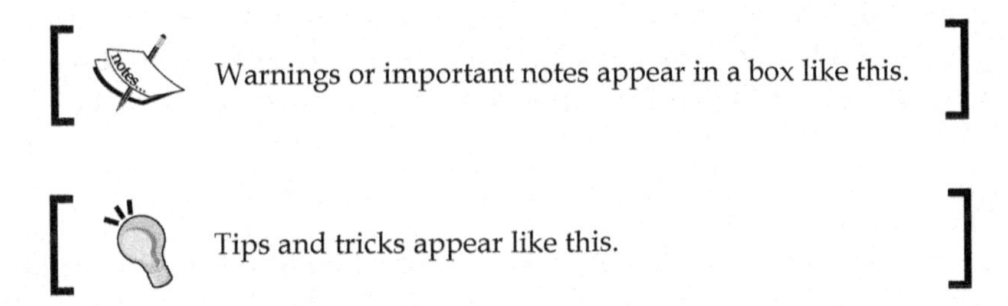

Warnings or important notes appear in a box like this.
Tips and tricks appear like this.

Reader feedback

Feedback from our readers is always welcome. Let us know what you think about this book—what you liked or may have disliked. Reader feedback is important for us to develop titles that you really get the most out of.

To send us general feedback, simply send an e-mail to `feedback@packtpub.com`, and mention the book title via the subject of your message.

If there is a topic that you have expertise in and you are interested in either writing or contributing to a book, see our author guide on `www.packtpub.com/authors`.

Customer support

Now that you are the proud owner of a Packt book, we have a number of things to help you to get the most from your purchase.

Downloading the example code

You can download the example code files for all Packt books you have purchased from your account at `http://www.packtpub.com`. If you purchased this book elsewhere, you can visit `http://www.packtpub.com/support` and register to have the files e-mailed directly to you.

Errata

Although we have taken every care to ensure the accuracy of our content, mistakes do happen. If you find a mistake in one of our books—maybe a mistake in the text or the code—we would be grateful if you would report this to us. By doing so, you can save other readers from frustration and help us improve subsequent versions of this book. If you find any errata, please report them by visiting `http://www.packtpub.com/submit-errata`, selecting your book, clicking on the **errata submission form** link, and entering the details of your errata. Once your errata are verified, your submission will be accepted and the errata will be uploaded on our website, or added to any list of existing errata, under the Errata section of that title. Any existing errata can be viewed by selecting your title from `http://www.packtpub.com/support`.

Piracy

Piracy of copyright material on the Internet is an ongoing problem across all media. At Packt, we take the protection of our copyright and licenses very seriously. If you come across any illegal copies of our works, in any form, on the Internet, please provide us with the location address or website name immediately so that we can pursue a remedy.

Please contact us at `copyright@packtpub.com` with a link to the suspected pirated material.

We appreciate your help in protecting our authors, and our ability to bring you valuable content.

Questions

You can contact us at `questions@packtpub.com` if you are having a problem with any aspect of the book, and we will do our best to address it.

1
Introduction to NativeScript

In this chapter, we are going to introduce you to Telerik's **NativeScript**, and discuss how NativeScript is totally unique in the cross-platform mobile device market, and how it is radically revolutionary for mobile **JavaScript** development. We will also walk you through the prerequisites of how to install the NativeScript command-line tool. Once the NativeScript tool is installed, we will walk you through the basic usage of the tool and briefly describe the most common parameters. Finally, we wrap up the chapter by creating and running our first NativeScript application.

In this chapter, we will be covering the following topics:

- What is NativeScript?
- NativeScript and TypeScript
- Common modules
- Installing NativeScript
- The NativeScript command line
- Creating your first application

NativeScript

If you are looking at this book, maybe you want to know why you should use NativeScript and what sets it apart from the crowded competition. Why shouldn't you use any of the other cross-platform tools? Let us dig in, and I'll explain why NativeScript is the answer to the best way of executing cross-platform mobile development.

Telerik's NativeScript

Telerik's NativeScript is a fairly new open source development system for creating cross-platform mobile applications almost entirely in JavaScript, with some optional CSS and XML to simplify developing the display layout. You can find the main location of each of the different projects that make up NativeScript at `https://github.com/NativeScript`. Even though it is new to the market, it is already fully compatible on Apple's iOS and Google's Android. In addition, Microsoft's Windows 10 Mobile is currently in development by Telerik, and others are working on Firefox Mobile. NativeScript uses the V8 engine (as used by Google Chrome and **node.js**) on Android and Apple's **JavaScriptCore** engine on iOS devices.

Other competitors

Now, there are several other competing JavaScript development systems for mobile devices. Some of these competitors have been established for a while. Other development systems may have large companies working on them. But neither of those will make any of the other tools the best choice. What makes NativeScript stand out from the crowd of other JavaScript environments is its unique design. Every other JavaScript environment requires a special bridge, or a compiled extension of some sort, which basically exposes some part of the native functionality of the host operating system to your JavaScript code. A lot of them are actually just web browsers wrapped in an application shell, so all the work you do is actually in a browser. If you decide you want Bluetooth on your iOS phone in one of the other products, you have to find someone who has made the iOS Bluetooth bridge or extension module in some other non-JavaScript language. In a lot of cases, you will even have to compile the module, and then you will still be hoping that the module has all the functionality you need.

NativeScript uniqueness

NativeScript is unique because it allows you to access the native elements of the host platform via JavaScript. In NativeScript, you can still see if someone has written a convenient JavaScript library to access the Bluetooth API. If so, since you understand JavaScript, you can easily make any changes you need. If not, then you can make your own JavaScript module to access all the host platforms of Bluetooth API. NativeScript is not a wrapper around a web view; it literally allows your JavaScript to work directly with the host platform APIs.

For example, to find out if a file exists, we can just call the native Android method in JavaScript:

```
var javaFile = new java.io.File('/some/file/name.ext');
var exists = javaFile.exists();
```

Or the native iOS Objective C code in JavaScript:

```
var fileManager = NSFileManager.defaultManager();
var exists = fileManager.fileExistsAtPath('/some/file/name.ext');
```

Since NativeScript allows you access to the full operating system libraries and third-party libraries from your JavaScript code, you do not need to wait for someone else to create a wrapper or bridge to talk to any part of any iOS or Android API. You can now fully use any of the APIs as a first-class citizen, which even includes using any new APIs when they are first released.

NativeScript allows you to be a fully first-class citizen; you have FULL access to the devices' entire released API from JavaScript. So anything that you can do in Android Java or iOS Objective C, you can now do directly in JavaScript.

NativeScript is easy

Now, before you get worried about having to know both iOS and Android to make your application, NativeScript has that covered. To simplify things, NativeScript already has a wide number of components, or modules, that wrap the most common things a developer will need, which are called the NativeScript common core modules. So, instead of having to write any Android or iOS specific code like I did above to see if a file exists, you can just write the following code:

```
var fs = require('file-system');
var exists = fs.File.exists(path);
```

The NativeScript filesystem module has each of the native platforms' API wrapped up so all you have to do is write to a common interface. But when you need to do something outside of the built-in modules and components, NativeScript is the only environment that allows you to easily have full access to everything the device offers right from JavaScript.

NativeScript and TypeScript

We are going to explain how parts of NativeScript are developed in **TypeScript** and what that means for you in terms of developing your awesome application using NativeScript.

What is TypeScript?

In 2012, Microsoft released an interesting language called TypeScript. This language is fully open sourced because the company felt it was something the JavaScript community needed. It is, in a nutshell, a superset of JavaScript with types and several other additional language features. If you write any code in TypeScript, you then have to use the TypeScript **transpiler** to convert the code from TypeScript back into JavaScript. One of the primary reasons people use TypeScript over regular JavaScript is that TypeScript offers the ability to do static type checking at the point it converts the code to JavaScript. So, you don't have a runtime hit, and you don't have to do a lot of runtime parameter checks if the code is all in TypeScript. This feature alone eliminates a type of bug that is very easy to access in JavaScript. In addition to static typing, it has several class/object type features that make inheritance and class definition considerably simpler and safer.

Types possess the ability to add markup to code denoting the type expected:

```
private validateMe(name: string, password: string):
boolean {  };
```

The `string` and `boolean` are declarations telling what the exact parameter types and expected return type are. This allows the transpiler to verify that the code matches the static types during the building stage.

Transpiler is a shortened term from translation compiler used to mean the code is converted from one language to another language. So, in this case, we are translating the code from TypeScript into JavaScript.

TypeScript's use in NativeScript

The NativeScript command-line utility, common modules, and components are all written in TypeScript. TypeScript is then transpiled to JavaScript before it is distributed for all us developers to download, install, and use. So, unless you are actually pulling the open source code from the NativeScript repositories, then all the code you will see is in JavaScript.

Fortunately for us, the majority of the differences between TypeScript and JavaScript are fairly minor, so the code transpiled to JavaScript in almost all cases is very close to the original TypeScript, which still makes it very readable.

Telerik just released a brand new module in v1.5.0 that will allow TypeScript to now be a first-class citizen in the development of your application. If you don't use this module, then you have to manually transpile all your TypeScript code each time before you build an application. After you execute a `nativescript install typescript` command, when the NativeScript command does anything with your code, it will automatically transpile all your TypeScript code first. This makes your development a much more streamlined process.

Choosing a development language

Since the final output of all the code must be JavaScript, you are able to write any of your applications or modules in TypeScript, **CoffeeScript**, or any other language that can be transpiled into JavaScript. This book is going to focus on doing everything in JavaScript as this is what the final code output must be for all the devices, and it is the common language that binds everything together.

Common modules

Common modules were created to solve the issue of JavaScript files polluting the global namespace with variables and functions that another JavaScript file could easily overwrite accidently. JavaScript allows you to redeclare or monkey patch your functions on a whim, which is part of what makes it so powerful. However, with that much power comes the ability to very easily shoot yourself in both feet simultaneously. Then, you are left scratching your head why you just lost both feet. To attempt to solve the issue of one included file function or variable being overwritten by another include file, developers came up with several techniques that evolved into the common module formats we use today. There are three standards available for you to use: the `CommonJS` module format, which is what `node.js` popularized; the `AMD` module format, which was designed for the asynchronous resolution of JavaScript files in a browser environment; and the brand new `ECMAscript 6` module format, which, when finally released, should become the de facto module format. All three of them wrap the source code so that none of the code in a module by default can interfere with the global namespace. NativeScript follows the `CommonJS` module format where you use `exports` and `module.exports` to tell what parts of the code in the module you want to expose to outside parties. When you see `var coolModule = require('cool-module');`, this is the syntax that the `CommonJS` module format uses to load a module.

Installing NativeScript

We are going to cover what you'll need for installation and development. Then, we will discuss how to install the NativeScript command, which you will use for anything relating to your NativeScript project.

Prerequisites

To get started on our journey of using NativeScript, we first must have several tools installed. The primary tool you will use for virtually everything is the `nativescript` command, or you can alternatively use the shorter alias of `tns` (short for Telerik NativeScript).

node.js

For the `nativescript` command to be installed and to make it work, you must first install `node.js`, which can be downloaded and installed from `https://nodejs.org/`. The `nativescript` command is also written in TypeScript and already pre-converted to JavaScript before you even download it. It uses `node.js` and several other common modules to perform all its work.

iOS

If you are planning on distributing your app on any iOS devices, you will need to have access to an Apple Macintosh platform. This is a requirement by Apple as they only allow you to compile and upload the app to the app store from a Macintosh. The Macintosh must have the Xcode and Xcode command-line tools installed. It is also highly recommended that you have an iPhone 4s or better to test at least the final application before you distribute it. The iOS emulator is not very accurate and because it gives you an idea of how your app will look, an actual device will accurately show you what your customers will see. The specific install instructions for iOS can be found at `http://docs.nativescript.org/setup/ns-cli-setup/ns-setup-os-x.html`.

Android

Android is a lot easier because you can execute development for Android on Linux, OSX, and Windows. For Android, you need to install Java JDK and then the Android SDK and tools. I also highly recommend that you install an optional third-party Android emulator rather than use the stock Android emulator. The third-party emulators are considerably faster than both the stock Android emulator and the add-on **Intel HAXM** emulator. The stock emulator and Intel HAXM can be downloaded via the Android SDK Manager. The instructions on the NativeScript site can walk you through installing all the tools that you will need for building and testing your application. The specific instructions for each of the platforms are located at `http://docs.nativescript.org/setup/quick-setup#the-nativescript-cli`.

Installation

Once you have `node.js` installed, you just need to do a simple `npm install -g nativescript` at a terminal shell (or known on Windows as a command prompt window). And then `npm` will download and install the required NativeScript code and command-line tool. It will install it globally so that it can be used from any project you are working on.

With the command path on Linux and Macintosh, the global commands are normally placed in `/usr/local/bin`, which is typically already in your path, so the `nativescript` command should work right away.

On Windows, unfortunately, you might have to add the path where `npm` installs the program globally. Type `nativescript` and see if it runs. If it fails to run, then you need to add npm's global directory to your path. Type `npm config get prefix` to get the current global directory.

Type `systempropertiesadvanced`, then click the **Environment Variables** button, then click on **PATH,** and finally, click the **Edit** button. Then, you can type a semicolon and add in the directory path to the all the `npm` global commands like the NativeScript command. So, your path might look something like this: `C:\windows;c:\windows\system;c:\program files (x86)\nodejs`.

Once the NativeScript command and required support tools are installed, you are all ready to begin developing NativeScript applications.

Installation help

Sometimes, getting NativeScript installed properly can be difficult because of all the differences between computers. Here are a couple places you can go to get help if you need it: `https://groups.google.com/forum/#!forum/nativescript` and `https://plus.google.com/communities/117408587889337015711`.

The NativeScript command line

Now, before we get to the creating a project part, let us have an overview of the commands available from the new `nativescript` command you just installed. If you forget any of these, you can easily type `nativescript` alone without any parameters to see a help screen at a console window, or type `nativescript /?` for a help screen in your browser.

NativeScript commands

These are just some of the most commonly used valid commands for the `nativescript` command. Several of these we will be covering as we progress in the book.

Command line	Description
`nativescript --version`	This returns the version of the `nativescript` command. If you are running an older version, then you can use `npm` to upgrade your `nativescript` command like this: `npm install -g nativescript`.
`nativescript create <your project name>`	This creates a brand new project.
`nativescript platform add <platform>`	This adds a target platform to your project.
`nativescript platform list`	This shows you what platforms you are currently targeting.

Command line	Description
`nativescript platform remove <platform>`	This command is normally not needed, but if you are messing with the platform directory and totally mess up your platform, you can remove and then add it back. Please note this deletes the entire platform directory, so if you have any specific customizations to your Android manifest or iOS Xcode project file, you should back it up before running the `remove` command.
`nativescript platform update <platform>`	This is actually a pretty important command. NativeScript is still a very active project under a lot of development. This command upgrades your platform code to the latest version, which typically eliminates bugs and adds lots of new features. Please note this should also be done with an upgrade of the common JavaScript libraries as most of the time, they also are typically in sync with each other.
`nativescript build <platform>`	This builds the application for that platform.
`nativescript deploy <platform>`	This builds and deploys the application to a physical or virtual device for that platform.
`nativescript emulate <platform>`	This builds and deploys the application to an emulator.
`nativescript run <platform>`	This builds, deploys, and starts the application on a physical device or an emulator. This is the command you will use the majority of the time to run your application and check out the changes.
`nativescript debug <platform>`	This builds, deploys, and then starts the application on a physical device or an emulator in debug mode. This is probably the second most used command.
`nativescript plugin add <plugin>`	This allows you to add a third-party plugin or component. These plugins typically include JavaScript based code, but occasionally, they might also contain an actual compiled Java or ObjectiveC library.

Command line	**Description**
`nativescript livesync - -watch`	This allows you to have the `nativescript` command watch for changes and automatically push them to the device. This is probably the third most used command if you are not using a better third-party **LiveSync** system. We call it LiveSync because it automatically syncs all your changes directly to the device in real time, without you having to rebuild the application. This speeds up your development of an application drastically.
`nativescript doctor`	This allows you to run some diagnostic checks on your environment if the `nativescript` command does not appear to be working.
`nativescript install`	This will (re)install any dependencies listed in your `package.json` file. The `package.json` file is typically modified by the plugin or library add function, so this is used typically to reinstall the plugins or libraries in the event you add a new platform or reinstall one.
`nativescript test [ init | <platform> ]`	This allows you to create or run any tests for your application. Using `init` will initialize the test framework for the application. Then, you just use the platform to run the tests on that platform.

Now that we have described some of the commands, let's use them to create your first mobile app via the `nativescript` command tool.

Creating your first application

I am going to walk you through how to create an application as it currently requires a couple steps that you need to do from a terminal shell. Then, we will show you how it looks.

Creating the application in easy steps

Creating a project is actually a fairly simple process; we are going to start by creating the application we will develop throughout this book.

1. Make sure you are at a terminal shell and then type:

   ```
   nativescript create crossCommunicator
   ```

2. This will create `crossCommunicator` as a subdirectory of the current directory you are running the `nativescript` command in. This new project directory will have all the required files for developing your project.
3. Next, you will need to switch to that new `crossCommunicator` directory that it created for you by typing:

   ```
   cd crossCommunicator
   ```

4. Then, type:

   ```
   nativescript platform add android
   ```

   And/or:

   ```
   nativescript platform add ios
   ```

5. To add each of the target environment(s), you will be compiling your app from this machine:

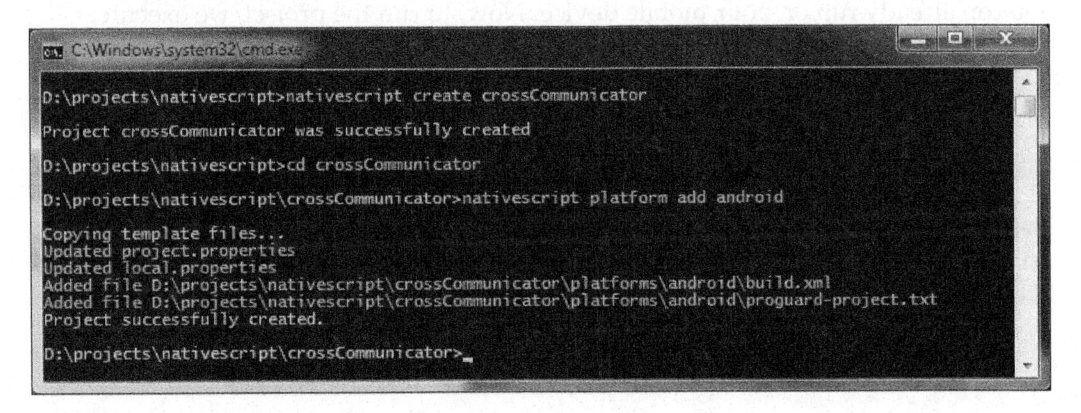

If everything worked properly, you should see something like the preceding image results.

Now, I personally do all my development on the Windows platform using JetBrain's wonderful cross-platform **PHPStorm** development environment. You are free to use any JavaScript editor you are comfortable with. Since I am using the Windows platform, I do the majority of my testing and debugging on the Android platform and emulator. The Android emulator is basically a full Android in your computer, so it behaves like an actual device. However, since I am also targeting iOS, every so often I also copy or sync the code from my Windows app folder to a Macintosh and then verify that everything looks good and works as expected on the iOS emulator and eventually an iOS device. The very first time when I copy my code over to a Macintosh, I use the `nativescript platform add ios` command as I need to add the iOS target on the Macintosh.

First time requirements

The very first time you create a project or add a platform, you do need an active Internet connection so the `nativescript` tool can download the current version of the runtime and platform libraries that it uses. In any future executions, it will first try to download the newest version, but if it fails, it will then use the currently cached version.

Running the app

With those simple steps, NativeScript creates a framework for an application that you can already run on your mobile device. Now, to run the project, we execute:

```
nativescript run android --emulator
```

Or:

```
nativescript run ios --emulator
```

NativeScript will then copy your application to the emulator, automatically start it up, and then you should see your first application running on the emulator screen like this:

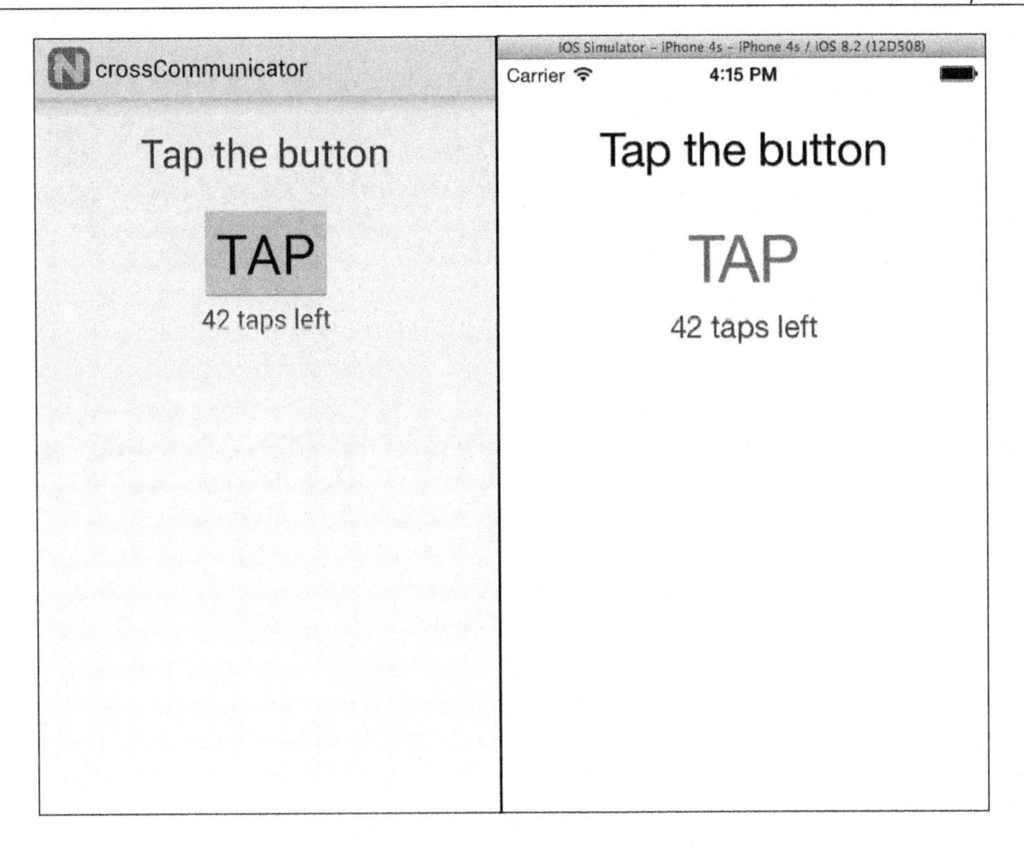

Summary

We covered a lot in this chapter. You learned what NativeScript is and what makes NativeScript unique among all the different JavaScript mobile development systems. You also learned how to install NativeScript and explored a large number of different command-line parameters you will use. And finally, you actually created and ran a new project.

Now you have the tools you need installed, and most importantly, we now have a running application. Let's dive into what makes the whole project tick. We will explore all the different files and folders for your project and gain an understanding of how each file is used, and finally, we will enhance the default application in *Chapter 2, The Project Structure*.

2
The Project Structure

In this chapter, I am going to show you how to navigate your new project and its full structure. I will explain each of the files that are automatically created and where you create your own files. Then, we will proceed to gain a deeper understanding of some of the base components of your application, and finally, learn how to change screens.

In this chapter, we will be covering the following topics:

- Project directory overview
- App directory overview
- NativeScript common core files
- Your application files
- An application page
- Foundational components
- Creating a second page
- Navigating between screens

Project directory overview

By running the `nativescript create crossCommunicator` command in the previous chapter, it created a nice structure of files and folders for us to explore.

If the NativeScript team has replaced the default project template since this book was written, the actual source code as it existed at the time of publishing is located in the book's source code repository found at `https://github.com/GettingStartedWithNativeScript/Chapter_1`. The `Example_1` folder contains the entire default template when this book was written. And you can clone it to your hard drive by running the `git clone https://github.com/GettingStartedWithNativeScript/Chapter_1` command and then proceeding to follow along inside the `Example_1` folder.

First, we will do a high-level overview of the different folders and their purposes and touch on any important files in those folders. Then, we will finish the overview by going into depth with the `App` directory, which is where you will spend pretty much all of your time when developing an application. To give you a good visual overview, here is what the project hierarchy structure looks like:

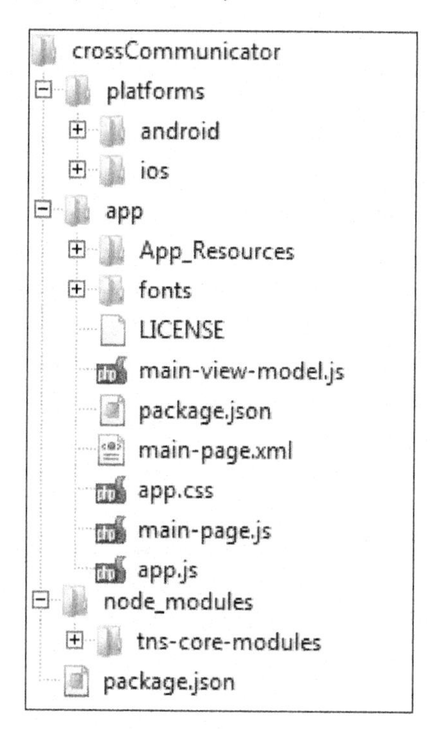

The root folder

In your `Root` folder, you will see only a couple directories, which we will describe below, and a single file. This file, `package.json`, will look something like this:

```
{
  "nativescript": {
    "id": "org.nativescript.crossCommunicator",
    "tns-android": {
      "version": "1.5.0"
    },
    "tns-ios": {
      "version": "1.5.0"
    },
  },
  "dependencies": {
    "tns-core-modules": "1.5.0"
  }
}
```

This is the NativeScript master project configuration file for your entire application. It basically outlines the basic information and all platform requirements of the project. It will also be modified by the `nativescript` tool when you add and remove any plugins or platforms. So, in the preceding `package.json` file, you can see I have installed the Android (`tns-android`) and iOS (`tns-ios`) platforms (using the `nativescript platform add` command), and they are both currently running at version 1.5.0. The `tns-core-modules` dependency was added by the `nativescript` command when we created the project, and it is the core module.

Changing the app ID

Maybe you want the app ID to be your company's name instead of the default ID of `org.nativescript.yourProjectName`, There are two ways to set the app ID. The first way is when you create the project, if you execute a `nativescript create myProjName --appid com.myCompany.myProjName` command, then this will automatically set the ID value. The second way, if you forgot to run the create with a `--appid` command, you can change this here. However, any time you change this, you will also have to remove all installed platforms and then re-add the platforms you are using. This must be done when each platform is added, because it uses the configuration ID while building any of the platform folders and any of the needed platform files.

The app folder

This folder contains all your code and resource files; we will go more in depth on these files in the next section as this is where you will be spending most of your time. This is also the main folder you should put under source control as it should contain all your application code and resources.

Source control. If you aren't using it, you really should be. Not only is it useful as a backup system, but it allows you to have a history of all the changes in your program. This ability comes in real handy when you change something and later realize you broke your program. With source control, you can compare the changes and revert only the part that broke. Another very useful feature is branching; you can create a branch of your project while you are working on a large feature and continue adding other features to your release version, then merge the branches when you are done. Suffice it to say, source control is awesome! You will notice that this book's source control is **Git**, but subversion is also an excellent option.

The lib folder

If your project requires it, then this folder is used during the build stage for the Android target; the `Android.jar`, the `android-support-v4.jar` and the `nativescript.jar` files, and any other added libraries are automatically copied into this folder during a run or build of your application for the Android platform. You can pretty much just ignore this folder since it is just used during building.

The hooks folder

This folder is created by the `nativescript` command if you install any additional modules that are `nativescript` command enhancements. This folder will contain the source code for the hooks so the `nativescript` command knows when and what to run. A couple of popular hooks are the `TypeScript` and `Protect` hooks. The `TypeScript` hook automatically compiles any TypeScript code into JavaScript before the application is built. This eliminates you having to manually do this step, and makes TypeScript a first-class citizen in the NativeScript ecosystem. The `Protect` hook minimizes and encrypts all your JavaScript code before the application is built; this gives you some piece of mind that your app won't just be literally copied.

The node_modules folder

This folder is used to store the NativeScript common core library module and any installed plugins. It is the folder where all master copies of the JavaScript source code for all the installed plugins reside. Why do I say master copies? Because another copy of the relevant source files is put into the platforms directory. The platform copy is what the build system uses for the actual building of your app. If you decide to change the platform copy and expect to see the changes, you will be quite disappointed as the `node_modules` files are re-copied into the `platforms` folder during a build.

In addition, if you want to look at how a plugin works, each plugin you install will have a subfolder with its name inside the `node_modules` folder.

> The reason this folder is called **node_modules** is because a very successful project called **node** made JavaScript common modules very popular. NativeScript uses `node` and node's package manager, `npm`, to do a lot of its project management. By NativeScript using `npm` to handle its plugins and core module, we then get the default `node_modules` folder.

The tns-core-modules folder

The `tns-core-modules` folder contains all the source code to the core common NativeScript modules. These modules are the glue that allows you to write common code that works on every platform. For example, if you execute a `var fs=require('file-system')` command, your application will load the filesystem JavaScript `tns-core-modules | file-system | file-system.js` file. If you look in this folder, you will see an Android and iOS version of this file; they both have the same interface that you will use, but they have the code to talk to the native filesystem on their respective platforms. The proper JavaScript version will be loaded automatically. As we progress through this book, we are going to go through several of these modules and show you how to use them properly. But for now, this is where all the common NativeScript modules reside if you need to find them. One minor thing to keep in mind is that the `tns-core-modules` folder also contains its own `package.json` file, which is what you can check to figure out the version of the common core components you have installed in your application project.

tns-core-modules and your own code

You should never put any of your own code in the `tns-core-modules` folder. This folder should be left strictly for the actual distributed Telerik NativeScript common core modules. This folder and everything in it will be deleted and/or replaced any time you upgrade the NativeScript common core components.

The platforms folder

This is where NativeScript puts all the specific platform code and libraries for each target platform that are needed for compiling your app for that specific platform. When you execute a `nativescript platform add android` command, you will see a folder called `Android` inside the `Platforms` folder. Any platform you add will have a subfolder with the same name inside the `Platforms` folder. You rarely have to enter these folders as they are almost completely taken care of by the `nativescript` command. However, there are several reasons you might have to work inside these folders. So, we will explore these reasons for each of the specific platforms.

Removing and upgrading platforms

If you execute a `nativescript platform remove platform` command, it fully deletes that specific platform folder and everything in it. So, if you have made any changes to the `AndroidManifest.xml` file or the iOS `.xcodeproj` file that you want to keep, you need to make sure to make a backup copy of these files first. In addition, when you do a platform upgrade, it also currently replaces your Xcode project files.

The platforms/android folder

One reason you might need to access the files in the `Platforms` folder is when you need to add or change any of the Android application permissions or any other application-wide change that needs to be made in the application's `AndroidManifest.xml` file. The `AndroidManifest.xml` file resides in the `Platforms/Android/src/main` folder. This is the only copy the build system uses. When you need to open and edit this file, you should see something like this:

```
1  <?xml version="1.0" encoding="utf-8"?>
2  <manifest xmlns:android="http://schemas.android.com/apk/res/android"
3      package="org.nativescript.crossCommunicator"
4      android:versionCode="1"
5      android:versionName="1.0" >
6
7     <supports-screens
8          android:smallScreens="true"
9          android:normalScreens="true"
10         android:largeScreens="true"
11         android:xlargeScreens="true"/>
12
13    <uses-sdk
14         android:minSdkVersion="17"
15         android:targetSdkVersion="22"/>
16
17     <uses-permission android:name="android.permission.READ_EXTERNAL_STORAGE"/>
18     <uses-permission android:name="android.permission.WRITE_EXTERNAL_STORAGE"/>
19     <uses-permission android:name="android.permission.INTERNET"/>
20
```

As you can see in the stock NativeScript, the `AndroidManifest.xml` file already has Internet permission on line 19, so we do not have to add this permission to our app later when we start using the Internet to communicate.

Currently in the works is a future version of NativeScript that will allow you to have the master copy of the `AndroidManifest.xml` file in your `App/App_Resources` folder. Then, you can maintain pretty much everything from inside your `App` folder. But, as it stands right now, any changes to the manifest file must be done to the version inside the `Platforms/Android/src/main` folder if you actually want them to work.

One precaution is that when you install any plugins, you should look at the `AndroidManifest.xml` file to verify that it didn't add any duplicate permissions. The `nativescript` command does not currently have any checks in place to verify that permissions are not duplicated. If you have any duplicate permissions, then the next time you compile or run your application, it may fail to start. Hopefully, in a newer version of NativeScript, this will be fixed so permissions are not duplicated, but in the meantime, if your app fails to start on Android, check to verify you don't have any duplicate permissions.

Bad resource files on Android

You will also have to navigate into the `Platforms/Android` folder if you add a file that already exists under the same name but has a different extension. For example, if you have a `button.jpg` image and you decide you want to optimize and compress it as `button.png`, this will break the build system when it sees both a `.jpg` and `.png` format of the same name. It will display an error at the command line listing the filename that is causing the issue, but you will still have to manually fix the issue. The two Android folders in which you will need to look for any offending resource files are `Platforms | Android | build | intermediates| res | merged | debug | ` and `Platforms | android | build | intermediates | res | merged | release`. Before compiling and running your application again, verify in your main `app | App_Resources` folder that it doesn't have the same duplicate name issue.

Compiled Android application location

The last and most important reason to enter the `Platforms | Android` folder is to get a copy of your compiled debug or release Android application APKs for distribution. Both the release and debug APKs are located in the `Platforms | Android | build | outputs | apk` folder.

The platforms/iOS folder

On the iOS side, you will actually have to edit the `Platforms | iOS | projectName.xcodeproj` project file for multiple reasons. NativeScript does not currently edit or change the iOS project file for you, so you have to manually do several parts of the configuration yourself. To edit the file, double-click on the application project file inside `Platforms | iOS`, and Xcode should open up with it and look something like this:

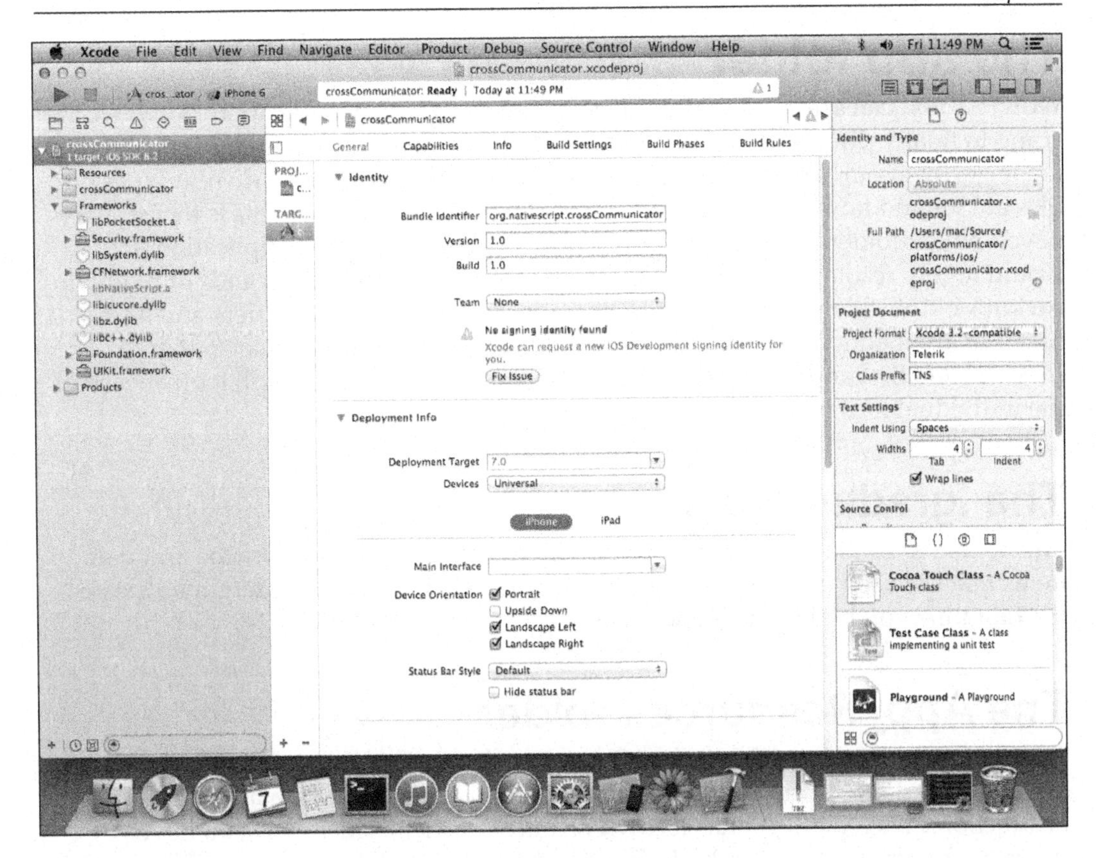

Currently, some of the changes you need to manually make are: adding your Apple developer key, adding any optional manually added libraries (**CocoaPods** are automatically added by the `nativescript` command), and making any other Xcode compilation changes you may want or need. The final and best reason you will have to use the Xcode project is to submit your application to the iOS application store. For more details on this, Apple has a developer guide at `https://developer.apple.com/library/ios/documentation/IDEs/Conceptual/AppDistributionGuide/SubmittingYourApp/SubmittingYourApp.html`.

The app folder

Wow! As you can see, a lot of stuff goes on just to create an application. Now, we are going to finally discuss the `App` folder structure; this folder is where we will spend the majority of our development time. We shall explore what the different types of files are for and how they are used to create an application. Since this is the primary development folder and contains your entire code base for your application, I would highly recommend you put this folder under source control and/or maintain backups of this folder. The `App` folder already contains a couple folders and a few files that are mentioned under the `App` folder files subsection. Let's look at both of these folders first and the files contained in them, and finally, we will look at each of the individual files in the `App` folder.

The .gradle folder

This folder is for the gradle build system; it basically only contains cache and data items that are used while the application is being built. This folder might be created the first time you build your application.

The App_Resources folder

This folder contains a subfolder for iOS and Android. This is one area where NativeScript does not currently offer you much in terms of cross-platform abstractions. Each platform has its own resource particularities, and you have to create the resources for each platform in the way the platform expects it. For example, in the `iOS` folder, you will see eight files that are all named variations of the default. These are all used as the launch screen resource for your iOS application. These eight screens are basically the same image, but are just different sizes, resolutions, or orientations. The same thing applies for the fourteen different icon files. These are all the same icon, and again, with just different resolutions and sizes. One place you can check out that can help with the app icons is `http://makeappicon.com/`.

Feel free to replace any of the images in the `App_Resources` folder with your own images to make the app your own. We will be covering more detailed information on the `App_Resources` folder and platform differences in *Chapter 6, Platform Differences*.

The fonts folder

The `fonts` folder doesn't actually exist, but if you want to use any cool fonts in your application, you just need to create the `fonts` folder inside your `App` folder and drop any truetype fonts you want to use in it. We will cover fonts a bit more in *Chapter 4, Building a Featured Application*.

The app folder files

We are now going to be looking at each of the files that are inside the `App` folder; these are the files you will change to make this your application. Let's start with the support files and finish with the actual files that make up the application page.

The package.json file

This file contains basic information about the current template that was installed. When you create a new application via the `nativescript create` command, this file, by default, copies everything from a template project called `tns-template-hello-world`. In the future, NativeScript will allow you to choose the template, but currently, this is the only template that is available and working. This template contains the folders we discussed and all the files we are about to discuss. This `package.json` file is from that template and basically tells you the template and the specific version of the template that was installed:

```
{
  "name": "tns-template-hello-world",
  "main": "app.js",
  "version": "1.5.0",
  ... more json documentation fields...
}
```

Feel free to modify this `package.json` file so that it matches your project's name and project details. This file does not currently serve much purpose beyond template documentation and the link to the `main` application file.

License

The `License` file that comes inside the `App` folder is the license the `tns-template-hello-world` file is under. In your case, your app will probably be distributed under a different license. You can either update this file to match your application's license or delete it.

App.js

Awesome! We have finally made it to the first of the JavaScript files that make up the code we will change to make this our application. This file is the `bootstrap` file of the entire application and where our fun begins. In the preceding `package.json` file, you can see that `package.json` references this file (`app.js`) under the `main` key. This key in the `package.json` file is what NativeScript uses to make this file the entry point for the entire application.

Looking at this file, we can see it is currently four simple lines of code:

```
var application = require("application");
application.mainModule = "main-page";
application.cssFile = "./app.css";
application.start();
```

The file seems simple enough, so let us work through the code as we see it. The first line loads the NativeScript common application component class; the application component wraps the initialization and life cycle of the entire application.

The `require()` function is the way you reference another file in your project; it will look in your current directory by default and then use some additional logic to look in a couple of places in the `tns_core_modules` folder to see if it can find the name as a common component.

Now that we have the application component loaded, the next lines are used to configure what the application class does when your program starts and runs. The second line tells us which one of the files is the main page. The third line tells the application which CSS file is the main CSS file for the entire application. And finally, we tell the application component to actually start. Now, in one sense, the application has actually started running; we are already running our JavaScript code. This `start()` function actually starts the code that manages the application life cycle and the application events, loads and applies your main CSS file, and finally, loads your main page files.

If you want to add any additional code to this file, you will need to put it before the `application.start()` command. On some platforms, nothing below the application.`start()` command will be ran in the `app.js` file.

App.css

This is the application-wide CSS file that provides you with a place to make any of your styles global for your entire application. If you remember, this file was specified as the application-wide CSS file on line three of the `app.js` file. We will cover how the NativeScript CSS works in the next chapter as there are some key differences between NativeScript CSS and the typical browser-based CSS. The good news is that for the most part, the NativeScript CSS works pretty close to what you would expect.

Application page

If you recall, in the `app.js` file, it had `application.mainModule = "main-page"` on line two. Notice that it does not specify a file extension. That is because you are telling the NativeScript runtimes in which you want it to try and load three different files that, if present, are all used together to make up a single page. For a page to automatically work properly, all three related files must be named with the exact same base name, just a different extension. We are going to discuss the main page of the application, but any and all pages are created exactly the same way. Let us proceed and look at the files that make up this page. One thing to keep in mind is that for a page to work, you must, at a minimum, have either the JS or XML page file.

The main-page.js file

The JavaScript portion of the page is probably where you will spend the majority of your time developing since it contains all the logic of your page. To create a page, you typically have a JavaScript file as you can do everything in JavaScript, and it is where all your logic for the page resides. In our application, the main page is currently only six lines of code:

```
var vmModule = require("./main-view-model");
function pageLoaded(args) {
  var page = args.object;
  page.bindingContext = vmModule.mainViewModel;
}
exports.pageLoaded = pageLoaded;
```

The first line loads the `main-view-model.js` file. If you haven't guessed yet, in our new application, this is used as the model file for this page. We will check out the optional model file in a few minutes after we are done exploring the rest of the `main-page` files.

An app page does not have to have a model; it is totally optional. Furthermore, you can actually combine your model JavaScript into the page's JavaScript file. Some people find it easier to keep their model separate, so when Telerik designed this example, they built this application using the MVVM pattern, which uses a separate view model file. For more information on MVVM, you can see the Wikipedia entry at `https://en.wikipedia.org/wiki/Model_View_ViewModel`.

This file also has a function called `pageLoaded`, which is what sets the model object as the model for this page. Line three assigns the page variable to the page component object that is passed as part of the event handler. Line four assigns the model to the current page's `bindingContext`. Then, we export the `pageLoaded` function as a function called `pageLoaded`.

Using `exports` and `module.exports` are the way we publish something to any other files that are using `require()` to load it. Each file is its own independent blackbox; nothing that is not exported can be seen by any of the other files. By using exports, you can create your interface of your code to the rest of the world. This is part of the CommonJS standard, and you can read more about it at the Node.js website.

The main-page.css file

This file actually does not exist in our new application, but you could create it and it would then provide CSS for just the main page. NativeScript automatically loads this file and applies it if it exists.

The main-page.xml file

This is the final file that is also named `main-page`; it is the page layout file. As you can see, the `main-page.xml` layout is a simple seven lines of XML code, which as you can see, actually does quite a lot:

```
<Page xmlns="http://www.nativescript.org/tns.xsd"
loaded="pageLoaded">
  <StackLayout>
    <Label text="Tap the button" cssClass="title"/>
    <Button text="TAP" tap="{{ tapAction }}" />
    <Label text="{{ message }}" cssClass="message"
    textWrap="true"/>
  </StackLayout>
</Page>
```

Each of the XML layout files are actually a simplified way to load your visual components that you want on your page. We will cover the XML Declarative UI in the next chapter, but in this case, it is what made your app look like this:

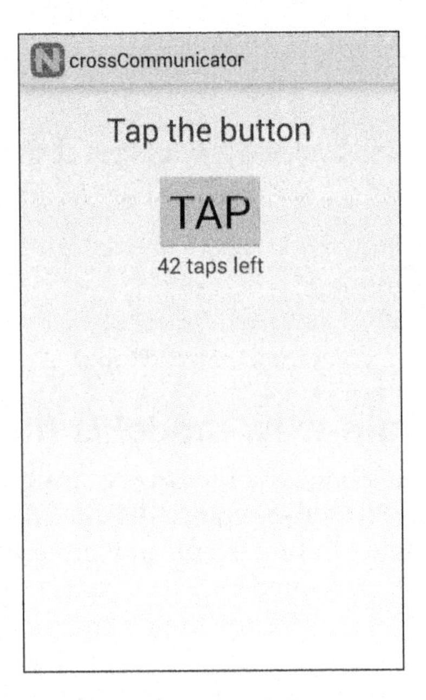

The main-view-model.js file

The final file in our tour of the `App` folder is the model file. This file has about 30 lines of code. And by looking at the first couple of lines, you might have figured out that this file was transpiled from TypeScript. Since this file actually has a lot of boilerplate and unneeded code from the TypeScript conversion, we will rewrite the code in plain JavaScript to help you easily understand what each of the parts are used for. This rewrite will be as close to the original as I can make it. So, without further ado, here is the original transpiled code to compare our new code with:

```
var observable = require("data/observable");
var HelloWorldModel = (function (_super) {
  __extends(HelloWorldModel, _super);
  function HelloWorldModel() {
    _super.call(this);
    this.counter = 42;
    this.set("message", this.counter + " taps left");
  }
```

```
    HelloWorldModel.prototype.tapAction = function () {
      this.counter--;
      if (this.counter <= 0) {
        this.set("message", "Hoorraaay! You unlocked the
        NativeScript clicker achievement!");
      }
      else {
        this.set("message", this.counter + " taps left");
      }
    };
    return HelloWorldModel;
  })(observable.Observable);
  exports.HelloWorldModel = HelloWorldModel;
  exports.mainViewModel = new HelloWorldModel();
```

Our rewrite of the main-view-model.js file

The rewrite of the `main-view-model.js` file is very straightforward; the first thing we need is for a working model to also require the `Observable` class; this is the primary class that handles data binding events in NativeScript. We then create a new instance of the `Observable` class named `mainViewModel`. Next, we need to assign the two default values. Then, we create the same `tapAction()` function, which is the code that is executed each time the user taps on the button. Finally, we export the `mainViewModel` model we created so it is available to any other files that require this file. This is what the new JavaScript version looks like:

```
// Require the Observable class and create a new Model from it
var Observable = require("data/observable").Observable;
var mainViewModel = new Observable();
// Setup our default values
mainViewModel.counter = 42;
mainViewModel.set("message", mainViewModel.counter + " taps
left");

// Setup the function that runs when a tap is detected.
mainViewModel.tapAction = function() {
  this.counter--;
  if (this.counter <= 0) {
    this.set("message", "Hoorraaay! You unlocked the NativeScript
    clicker achievement!");
  } else {
    this.set("message", this.counter + " taps left");
  }
};
```

```
// Export our already instantiated model class as the variable
name that the main-page.js is expecting on line 4.
exports.mainViewModel = mainViewModel;
```

Pretty much the only thing that is not totally self-explanatory or explained in this code is the `set()` command. What is probably fairly obvious is that this command sets the variable specific to the value specified. However, what is not obvious is when a value is set on an instance of the `Observable` class, it will automatically send a change event to anyone who has asked to be notified of any changes to that specific variable. If you recall, in the `main-page.xml` file, with the line `<Label text="{{ message }}" ....>`, when the layout system creates the label, it will automatically register the label component as a listener for all change events on the `message` variable. Now, every time the `message` variable is changed, the text on this label changes. We will be discussing more about observables and binding in the following chapter.

Foundational components

Now that we have explored all the project files that were automatically created for you, let's examine several foundational components that have already been referenced in the main page. These components are the glue of the application, and without them, we would have no application.

Application component

If you recall, earlier in the chapter, we discussed the `app.js` file. It basically contains only the code that is responsible for setting up the properties of your application and then finally, it starts the application component. So, you probably have guessed that this is the primary component for your entire application lifecycle. Part of the features that this component provides us with is access to all the application-wide events. Frequently, in an app, you will want to know when your app is no longer the foreground application or when it finally returns to being the foreground application. To get this information, you can attach to two of the events that it provides like this:

```
application.on("suspend", function(event) {
  console.log("Hey, I was suspended - I thought I was your
  favorite app!");
});
application.on("resume", function(event) {
  console.log("Awesome, we are back!");
});
```

Some of the other events you can watch from the application component are `launch`, `exit`, `lowMemory`, and `uncaughtError`. These events allow you to handle different application-wide issues that your application might need to know about.

Frame component

The frame component is the logical view that controls which page is seen. The frame component only has a couple of functions and properties since it is used to load new pages or return to prior pages. This is one of the few components for which you do not typically need to create a new component of its type. In this case, you typically access the top frame via the special `topmost()` singleton function and then call any and all frame functions from that main frame object. The primary methods you will be using are the `navigate(pageName)`, which is what will load a new page, and the `goBack()` function, which is what returns you to the prior page. The only other function you might use frequently is the function `canGoBack()`, which you can use to find out if you can go back any more pages. We will be using these functions later in this chapter.

Page component

The page component is what wraps up the entire page and provides all the page life cycle events for each of the pages. Earlier, we explored the three files that make up a page, but we will now check out the actual page component that uses those three files and what it does for us. Part of the job of the page component is that it provides events for things like loading, navigating, and unloading of pages. If you recall, we had a `pageLoaded()` function exported on the `main-page.js` file. This function is actually tied to a `loaded` event, which is fired from this component when the actual main page is loaded. The `loaded` event allowed us, in this case, to set up a model for the main page. Since your code for this page is now running, you can use the loaded event to set up any other logic you might also need at the start of your page before it is visible to the user. In addition, all the page events also give you access to the page component as part of the event parameter, which can be used to configure any other page component changes. Some of the other events that the page component manages for you are the unloaded, navigating (to and from), navigated (to and from), and `shownModally` events.

> These events are fired in the following sequence when you start to navigate to a new page:
>
> - Old page fires its `navigatingFrom` event
> - New page fires its `navigatingTo` event
> - Old page fires its `navigatedFrom` event
> - Old page fires its `unloaded` event
> - New page fires its `loaded` event
> - New page fires its `navigatedTo` event
>
> If you are showing a page modally, the events are:
>
> - New modal page fires its `loaded` event
> - New modal page fires its `shownModally` event
> - New modal page fires its `unloaded` event
> - The original page is now in the `callback` function you provided when you called the `showModal` method

As you can see, you have access to quite a bit of the life cycle of both the page you are leaving and the page you are now loading. Beyond the events the Page component offers, it also contains some basic properties like the actual `actionBar` property, which allows you access to the `actionBar` component and all its functions, properties, and methods. And finally, it has several methods like the `addCss` function, which allows you to add CSS programmatically to the page, and a `showModal` function, which allows you to load another page to show modally over the current page. The Page component, like all other visual components, is a descendant of the View component, so it also contains all the same View properties, methods, and functions as any other View descendants do. We will be discussing the View component in the next chapter.

Creating a second page

Now that we have an idea of all the project files and foundational components, why don't we do something cool and finish off this chapter by creating a brand new page and then using our newfound skills to navigate to it?

Creating additional files and pages

Some people might prefer individual subdirectories per page or some other project layout scheme. NativeScript has no issues with you creating your project system the way you want. For our project, and to keep things simple, we are just going to add any new files to our main app directory. To create a new page, we just need to create the files associated with a page. So, in this case, we need to create a single new file called `settings.js` in our main `App` folder. And then, finally, we need to make a change to the `main-view-model.js` file to show our new page.

Creating settings.js

In our application, we are going to need a settings page, so we are going to create the framework for our application settings page right now. We are going to just get our feet a little wet and explore how to build it purely in JavaScript. As you can see, the following code is fairly straightforward. First, we require all the components we will be using: Frame, Page, StackLayout, Button, and finally, the Label component. Some of these components we have discussed already; the rest we will be covering in the next chapter. Then, we have to export a `createPage` function, which is what NativeScript will be running to generate the page if you do not have an XML layout file to go along with the page's JavaScript file. At the beginning of our `createPage` function, we create each of the four components we will need. Then, we assign some values and properties to make them have some sort of visual capability that we will be able to see. Next, we create the parent-child relationships and add our label and button to the Layout component, and then we assign that layout to the Page component. Finally, we return the page component:

```
// Add our Requires for the components we need on our page
var frame = require("ui/frame");
var Page = require("ui/page").Page;
var StackLayout = require("ui/layouts/stack-layout").StackLayout;
var Label = require("ui/label").Label;
var Button = require("ui/button").Button;

// Create our required function which NativeScript uses
// to build the page.
exports.createPage = function() {
  // Create our components for this page
  var page = new Page();
  var layout = new StackLayout();
  var welcomeLabel = new Label();
  var backButton = new Button();
```

```
    // Assign our page title
    page.actionBar.title = "Settings";
    // Setup our welcome label
    welcomeLabel.text = "You are now in Settings!";
    welcomeLabel.cssClass = "message";

    // Setup our Go Back button
    backButton.text = "Go Back";
    backButton.on("tap", function () {
      frame.topmost().goBack();
    });

    // Add our layout items to our StackLayout
    layout.addChild(welcomeLabel);
    layout.addChild(backButton);

    // Assign our layout to the page.
    page.content = layout;
    // Return our created page
    return page;
  };
```

One thing I did want to mention here is that if you are creating a page totally programmatically, without the use of a Declarative XML file, the `createPage` function must return the Page component. The Frame component is expecting to have a Page component.

Navigating to another page

The final piece is navigating to the new settings page we just created. You will need to open up your `main-view-model.js` file. We are going to change the `tapAction` function to navigate to our new page. At this point, you may already know exactly what to do since we have already described what the Frame component is used for and written code to use the Frame's `goBack()` function. So, if you would like to take a break from reading and see if you can handle this, please feel free to enhance the app to navigate to the new settings page. La...la...la... la...oh, you're back? Well, did it work? If not, or you are just curious about how I would do it, let's proceed. We should insert this next piece of code as the very first line: `var frame = require('ui/frame');`. This line will give us access to the Frame object. Then, as the first line inside the `tapAction` `if` statement, I would add the following code: `frame.topmost().navigate('settings');`. With those two changes, the application will now show the settings screen when you tap on the **Tap** button on the main screen.

Running the application

You typically use the `nativescript run` command to have NativeScript build, deploy, and launch your application on a device or emulator all in one step. However, you usually need to provide a couple of additional parameters to tell the command which device you want to deploy your app to and then run it on. The first thing you need to append to the command is which platform. So, if you are running this on an iOS device, you would type `tns run ios`, and Android would likewise be `tns run android`. Most of the time, though, you will be targeting an emulator, so you will also want to append the `--emulator` to the command line. For iOS, this would be `tns run ios --emulator`, which will automatically launch the default iOS simulator and run your application inside it. Android is the same; when you add the `--emulator` command, it will launch the default Android emulator.

One side note is that since you can have multiple emulators, you can choose which emulator you want to use on iOS by using the `--device <devicename>` command, and you can do the same for Android by using the `--avd <devicename>` or `--geny <devicename>` commands. You can get the devices on iOS by running `nativescript emulate ios --available-devices`, and for Android, you can run `android list avd` or `genyshell -c "device list"`.

To simplify launching things, I typically create a batch file or a shell script called `go` in which I put the complete launch string so I don't have to type in the entire device name, as the device names can be really long. Then, all I have to do is type `go` to run my project.

Viewing our screen

Run the app by typing the `nativescript run` command with its parameters.

And then, click the **Tap** button and you should see our brand new settings screen:

Before you tap the **Go Back** button, can you surmise why the button is so large from the information presented in this chapter? If not, don't worry; we will cover the answer in the next chapter.

Summary

We have covered a large amount of foundational information in this chapter. Not only did we go through all the project files that were created by the `tns create crossCommunicator` command, but we also covered which files are used for your application and where to find and make any changes to the project control files. In addition, we also covered several foundational components such as the Application, Frame, and Page components. And we walked through the three different files that make up an application page. Finally, we created a new page and navigated to it and back from it.

In the next chapter, we are going to cover several more components and explore the XML Declarative UI and flesh out binding and observables, working with events, and styling your application with CSS.

3
Declarative UI, Styling, and Events

Since we want to produce sleek and nice-looking applications, we are going to investigate the Declarative UI and its styling system in this chapter. In addition, we are going to explore several of the most frequently used common components and the event system. Finally, we'll wrap up the chapter by actually styling the main screen.

In this chapter, we will be covering the following topics:

- The Declarative UI
- Using the Declarative UI for our Settings page
- Binding and events
- Styling the UI
- Trying out and styling our application

Declarative UI

We are going to look at how the Declarative UI makes our lives much simpler in that we typically only have to create a single XML file to cover the way our app looks on all the platforms.

In this section, we will be exploring how the XML system works behind the scenes. We'll dissect more components, check out the event system, and finally, look at the component hierarchy and what it offers us. So, let us dive right into the `main-page.xml` file and figure out how it all works.

XML parser

Whoa! Bet you thought we were going to dive right into the `main-page.xml` file, didn't you? Well, not so fast; we have to take a small detour. We need to look at how the XML parser works to understand what is going on when NativeScript handles a Declarative UI XML file. So, let's get this show on the road.

Now, if you are coming from an HMTL background, you can probably teach me some really cool HTML tricks. But, since all of us are not so blessed, we will cover it for those who aren't familiar with any HTML or XML. An XML parser handles an XML file by breaking everything down into nodes. A node is what is between the less than (<) and greater than (>) symbols, for example, `<I am a Node>`. To close a `<Node>`, we use the forward slash (/) character.

So, a standalone node would be `<Wow />`, with the slash at the end before the closing greater than symbol. To create a node with other nodes inside it, you'd use `<Wow>... <other nodes>...</Wow>`. Each node in the XML is then broken down into individual parts. The first part of the node is the element, or in NativeScript, the UI component. The rest of the node is used as properties for that UI component. One thing to keep in mind is that all the elements and properties are case-sensitive. Breaking this down, if I have `<Hello talk="true"><Hi we="are awesome" /></Hello>`, then the NativeScript parser will basically do the following:

```
var Hello = require('ui/hello');
var hello = new Hello();
hello.talk = true;
var Hi = require('ui/hi');
var hi = new Hi();
hi.we = "are awesome";
hello.addChild(hi);
```

Now, as you can see, NativeScript requires and creates each of the components, assigns all the properties and events, and then finally, handles configuring any parent-child relationships. This saves us a lot of time and enhances your readability of the screen UI. Now that we have a grasp on what is happening behind the scenes, shall we proceed to looking at our `main-page.xml` file?

```
<Page xmlns="http://www.nativescript.org/tns.xsd"
loaded="pageLoaded">
  <StackLayout>
    <Label text="Tap the button" cssClass="title"/>
    <Button text="TAP" tap="{{ tapAction }}" />
    <Label text="{{ message }}" cssClass="message"
    textWrap="true"/>
  </StackLayout>
</Page>
```

This file looks familiar; we took a peek at this file briefly in the previous chapter. How about we finally break down exactly what this file does for us? Let us look at what happens with each component.

Page, StackLayout, label, and more

Since we are going to look at each of these components from the perspective of the XML parser, I would like to reinforce that each of these components are actually all JavaScript code and can be fully controlled by your JavaScript code. So, let's get started and look at the first XML node.

<Page ...> node

You will notice the entire XML file is wrapped in or contains a root XML element `<Page>` node. If you recall in *Chapter 2, The Project Structure*, we had to create a new Page component to wrap everything in when we made the `settings.js` page. This is how we create the Page component in Declarative UI. Each of the nodes in the file is defining a new component. The rest of this Page node `<Page xmlns="http://www.nativescript.org/tns.xsd" loaded="pageLoaded">` declaration is page properties and events.

One side note: the default `xmlns` property is not actually a real property on the Page component. It's actually not a real property on anything. This is the only property in the Declarative UI that is really a totally bogus property. It is not an actual property on the Page control, so it's not visible from JavaScript. Instead, it is used to configure the XML parser on how to allow access to additional third-party component folders. You can link to another component folder by executing `xmlns:MyCustomControls = "path | to | my | controls"`, and then you can reference a control in that folder by executing `<MyCustomControls:controlName>`. The `MyCustomControls` instance can be any name you want, so you could just as easily have `xmlns:controls="my | controls/"` and then use `<controls:controlName>`. Oh, and the default `xmlns` is currently totally ignored by the parser, so you can actually eliminate it from your XML file if you want, unless your editor uses it to provide autocorrect and intelligent typing ability. We will cover more on how to use this in *Chapter 5, Installing Third-Party Components*.

As you might have surmised, the `loaded` property in the XML is actually the `loaded` event, which we discussed in regards to the Page component in *Chapter 2, The Project Structure*. If you have not surmised yet, we are telling the parser that it needs to hook up our `pageLoaded` function that we declared and exported in the `main-page.js` file to this Page component's `loaded` event.

<StackLayout ...> node

You will notice that the next component, which is inside the `<Page>` node, is the `<StackLayout>` node. Since it is inside the `Page` node, it will make this a child of the Page component. Since a Page component can only have a single child, we then have to use one of the Layout components to allow us to have multiple children.

> Technically, a Page component can have two XML children. The first is the ActionBar; this is behind the scenes and is automatically assigned to the `ActionBar` property on the Page. So, in the XML it looks like a child, but programmatically it is actually assigned to a property, and your child count will always be `0` or `1` depending on if you add any other controls that will actually be a child of the Page component. If you are building or accessing the page programmatically, you will need to access or assign the `ActionBar` property and not try to use it as a child.

We will cover all the different styles of layouts and how to mix and match them properly in *Chapter 4, Building a Featured Application*. Moving right along, the StackLayout is one of the simplest layouts. Concisely, the children will either stack everything horizontally or by default, stack everything vertically. This makes it one of the more commonly used layouts. In our case, it has three children that will all be stacked vertically one right after another.

> To change the StackLayout orientation, you use the `orientation` property and set it to `horizontal` for a horizontal layout. This would be accomplished this way: `<StackLayout orientation="horizontal">`.

<Label ...> node

The Label `<Label text="Tap the button" cssClass="title"/>` is the next component we are declaring, and you will notice it is the first of the children of the StackLayout. This means it will be first on the screen. The Label is probably the most common component as it is used to display a line or multiple lines of text on the screen.

> If you need to display HTML text, use the `HtmlView` component instead of the Label component.

The Label component offers us a couple of properties and methods; the primary property you will be using is the `.text` property or the `.formattedText` property to set what the label says. In this case, we are using the `.text` property to make the label say "**Tap the button.**".

The second property defined in our Label is the `.cssClass` property, in which we assign the value of "**title.**" We will learn later on in this chapter about the `cssClass` property and how it is used.

Before we forget, we should look briefly at the `.formattedText` property. It allows you to pass in a fully pre-formatted `FormattedString` component rather than just a straight text string. We are going to venture down a small bunny trail here to try to teach you a new concept. The `.formattedText` property gives me a great place to teach you an important new concept in the Declarative UI.

FormattedString component

This non-visual component allows you to create spans of text that each have their own different formatting. For instance, let's pretend the following `<Label>` XML was in our `main-page.xml` file in place of the above `<Label>` component:

```
<Label class="title">
  <Label.formattedText>
    <FormattedString>
      <FormattedString.spans>
        <Span text="Tap the" fontSize="10"/>
      <Span text="button" fontAttribute="Bold"/>
      </FormattedString.spans>
    </FormattedString>
  </Label.formattedText>
</Label>
```

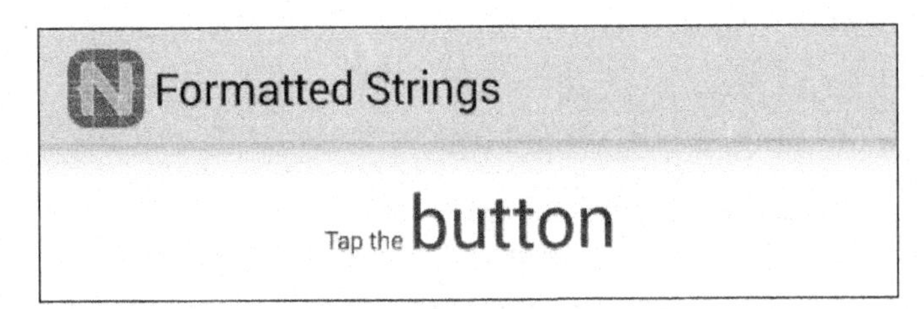

You can probably guess that the Label will still say **Tap the button**. However, **Tap the button** will be in 10-point font, and the **button** will be in a bolded default font size. Since a picture is worth a thousand words, the above picture is what it would look like.

The `FormattedString` component currently supports changing the `fontSize`, `fontAttribute` (bold and italic), `fontFamily`, `foregroundColor`, `backgroundColor`, `underline`, and `strikethrough` properties. Pretty cool, huh? You might be wondering, "hey, where is the new concept you promised me?" Well, I have not forgotten. Pay close attention and look at the XML I wrote previously, and you might notice that the XML tags I wrote are a bit different from any other Declarative UI XML we have looked at. It has some periods in some of the component names. As our new concept, this is how the Declarative UI deals with any complex component properties.

Complex properties

"What is a complex property?" you ask. A **complex property** is when you are creating, modifying, or assigning a subcomponent of the current component. Let us break this XML down:

- `<Label>`: This is just like any other XML nodes we have looked at. We are just creating a new Label component.
- `<Label.formattedText>`: This is the first complex property. This XML is not creating a component; instead, it is doing an assignment. It is saying use the parent component (in this case, the Label), and its property, `.formattedText`. This is assigning everything inside this node to the `.formattedText` property.
- `<FormattedString>`: We are creating a brand new `FormattedString` component, which is what is assigned to the Label `formattedText`.
- `<FormattedString.spans>`: The fourth declaration is another complex property that will use the `FormattedString.spans` property for everything inside itself.
- `<Span>`: The fifth and sixth lines create two new Span components as usual, which are then assigned as the children to the `FormattedString.spans` property.

Or, in JavaScript, the assignments would be:

```
var label = new Label(); // <Label>
var formattedString = new formattedString() // <FormattedString>
var span1 = new Span(); // <Span>
var span2 = new Span(); // <Span>
formattedString.spans = [span1, span2]; // <FormattedString.spans>
label.formattedText = formattedString; // <Label.formattedText>
```

The rest of the XML tags are just closing tags, so we will skip them. By using complex properties, this allows you access to any subcomponents of a component and gives you the ability to make changes and/or assignments. There is an enhancement request in the NativeScript project on how to simplify complex properties in the Declarative UI. By the time this is published and you actually read this section, there is a strong possibility that complex properties will also support a much more simplified system, perhaps something like this:

```
<Label>
  <FormattedString>
  <Span text="Tap the" fontSize="10"/>
  <Span text="button" fontAttribute="Bold"/>
  </FormattedString>
</Label>
```

Under this proposal, the simplified XML would work like this. The Label already knows the only complex property it has is the `formattedText`, and the only property that takes a `FormattedString` is the `formattedText` property. When the Declarative UI parser attempts to add the `FormattedString` to the Label as a child, the Label automatically assigns it to the `formattedText` property based on either one of the above two criteria. The same thing goes for when the Declarative UI parser attempts to assign the Span components to the `FormattedString` property; the `FormattedString` property knows the only complex property it has that takes a Span component is the `Spans` property.

So, by adding a bit of smarts to the Declarative UI parser, this would optionally allow us to eliminate a lot of the extra unnecessary Declarative UI code on any complex properties.

Now that we have wandered down the path of complex properties, shall we resume manually parsing our original `main-page.xml` file?

<Button ...> node

The next child of the StackLayout is the Button component,`<Button text="TAP" tap="{{ tapAction }}" />`. The Button is another very common component; you almost always have to click or tap somewhere on the screen to do some sort of action. In addition to the `tap` event, the Button component also has both a `text` and a `formattedText` property, which work just like the Label component.

In the preceding XML, you can see that the Button component has the `tap="{{ tapAction }}"` property. The double braces (or curly brackets) *{{ }}* in a property mean that this property uses binding to attach the `tap` event. In this case, the binding system will bind the Button's `tap` event to the `tapAction` function on the `main-page-model.js` file. We will discuss more about binding later in this chapter when we discuss the Binding component.

Second <Label...> node

The final child of the StackLayout is another Label node: `<Label text="{{ message }}" cssClass="message" textWrap="true"/>`. This label also uses binding like the button, but in this case, it is binding the `text` property to the message value on the `main-page-model.js` exported class.

The other property in this example is the `textWrap` property. This allows you to choose if the text is truncated or wrapped, as shown in this image:

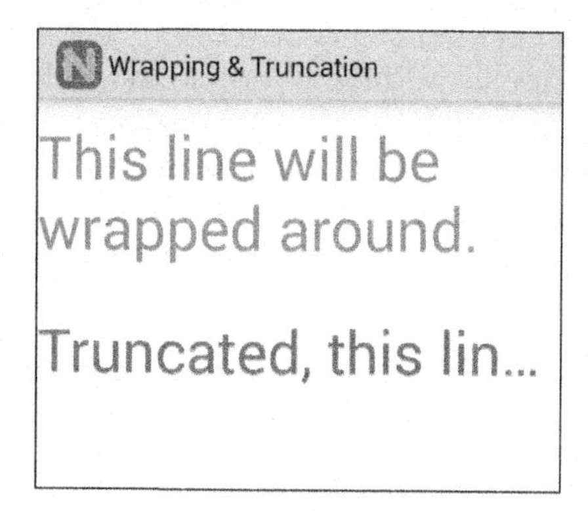

Since the rest of the `main-page.xml` file is just closing tags, we are going to jump to another made-up example file to learn another important Declarative UI technique.

Declarative UI and components

As you can see, the Declarative UI is quite expressive. It allows you to handle any visual layout you might need. It is also fully cross-platform, so your UI works on each of the supported platforms. It makes designing the screen easy to do with very little code. However, I wanted to reinforce again that all these UI declarations are JavaScript components. You can do all of this via JavaScript, and at any point, you can still change any of the components' properties during runtime.

Visual components

All the visual components that you use in the Declarative UI actually have a large list of methods, properties, and events that are inherited from the View component. For a list of methods and properties, see: `http://docs.nativescript.org/ApiReference/ui/core/view/View.html`. This inheritance is what allows us to do nifty things like `myButton.on('tap', function() { ... do something... });` since the `on()` method is inherited.

Using the Declarative UI for our settings page

Since we have now learned how the Declarative UI works, it should be a simple task to convert our JavaScript version, which we created in *Chapter 2, The Project Structure*, into a Declarative UI version. Let's see if you can accomplish this on your own. If you get stuck or just want to verify, please feel free to see how I did it. Let us start by creating a new `settings.xml` file.

Our settings.xml file

Let us see how much we have learned. I will ask a question, and you determine if you can answer it.

- The first thing we need to do is create the _____ component. Yes, you are totally correct; the Page component is always first. Now, this next one is going to be tricky.
- The next component you need is ____. If, you said StackLayout, you are close—the StackLayout will be needed, but we have one other component property that should actually come before it. You might want to read the source code to the `settings.js` file again to see if you can figure it out. Don't worry, I'll wait patiently.
- So, you need a _____? If you said `Page.actionBar`, you would be totally correct. You figured out that little curveball of mine in the source code. We needed a complex property to assign the title to an `actionBar` subcomponent. Uh oh, another tricky spot! Think back to our complex properties discussion; do you think you can guess what tag you need now?
- We need a ______? ActionBar. Awesome, you noticed—when dealing with any complex properties, the majority of the time a subcomponent is named the same as the property. Now comes another tricky one.

- What do we need now _____? Hah, did I get you on this one? Or did you figure out that we need the closing `page.actionBar` tag?
- Finally, we need the _____? `StackLayout` tag.
- Following that, we need a ______? Yes, you are correct, a Label.
- Then, we need one more component, the ______? Yep, it is the `Button`. For simplicity's sake, let's name the tap listener to tap on the button. And then, we can put in the rest of our closing tags.

If you skipped the `page.ActionBar` tag in our questions and just used the `ActionBar` tag, this is also correct usage for the Page component. Normally, you need to use complex properties to access a property. The Page component actually has some additional code while it is being built, and so if you use an `ActionBar` component as a child, it automatically gets assigned as the page `ActionBar` property. Using this complex property is more semantically correct as it shows you that it is a property and not a child, but both methods work the same way.

Our new `settings.xml` file should look like this:

```
<Page>
  <Page.actionBar>
    <ActionBar title="Settings" />
  </Page.actionBar>
  <StackLayout>
    <Label text="We are now in the settings!" cssClass="message"
    />
    <Button text="Back" tap="tap" />
  </StackLayout>
</Page>
```

You might have noticed in the preceding Declarative UI setting page that we used `<Button text="Back" tap="tap">` rather than the `{{ tapAction }}` property that is present in the main page. The reason is that on the settings page, we are not using a binding model; we are telling the Declarative UI to use the `tap` function exported in the `settings.js` file. On the main page, it is using the binding system to bind to the `tapAction` function that the model exports.

Awesome! Now, our XML file, when we run it, should look exactly like our pure JavaScript version did from the last chapter. However, now we need to modify the `settings.js` file since it is also going to create the same interface before the XML even loads. Do you think you can modify the `settings.js` file to make it work properly now? Here are a couple of hints:

- In our preceding code, we set the `button.tap = "tap"` property
- You only need one `require()` statement
- The file should be two or four lines long
- You only need one function, which only contains a single line of code

Hopefully, you wrote something like this:

```
var frame = require("ui/frame");
exports.tap = function() {
  frame.topmost().goBack();
};
```

This code is simple; you need to require the frame component because we use the `goBack()` method from the frame. You also need to export the `tap` function, since the UI is going to be looking for an exported `tap` function to be in the `settings.js` file. And, of course, in the `tap` function we need to run the actual `goBack()` command.

Your next step is to do a `nativescript run android --emulator` execution and check out our brand new XML version of the settings screen. I want to point out that the XML version and the new `Node.js` code work identically; however, we went from around 40 lines of pure JavaScript code to nine lines of XML and four lines of JavaScript. This ends up being a lot smaller and much easier to enhance and maintain.

Binding and event system

We are going to change gears for a few minutes to touch on two other related topics that not only affect the Declarative UI, but your whole application. You need to be able to respond to any event, like finger touches, downloads completing, and the application being stopped. In addition to the event system, a related subject is binding, as binding typically handles part of the event automatically. So, let's dig into these two areas of NativeScript.

Event system

While we have already touched briefly on one use of the `Observable` component when we discussed the model file in *Chapter 2, The Project Structure*, let us go more in-depth on this component.

This component has two similar responsibilities; both deal with events. First, this class is used as the source class for using any variables that need binding.

By source, I mean this is the class that provides the memory location for you to store your variables that you want to stay in sync with other components and your code. For example, if you look at our created `main-view-model.js` property that we discussed in *Chapter 2, The Project Structure*, it uses the Observable component for the `counter` variable and the `tapAction`. This is the source class for tracking our `counter` variable. The other components and your own code can also listen for `propertyChange` events. This event is fired, which allows you to react anytime that property or variable is changed. The NativeScript components, when bound, automatically listen for that event and will update themselves every time that variable changes. This also is frequently two-way, so that when the component value changes, it changes the source variable. You can use the `set` and `get` methods to create, change, and view these variables.

The second responsibility of this component is that it is the entire event system. Yes, you read that correctly. This component is the entire event system for the application. If you are listening to an event, it is because of this component. You can easily listen to any event you want and then anywhere else in your code, fire a notification for that event. This component handles all of it. The Observable component is fully responsible for tracking every one of the events and each of the events' callback listeners.

The methods the Observable component publishes for subscribing to an event are the `on` or `attachEventListener` listener. Then, to stop listening to any event, you can use the `off` or `removeEventListener` listener.

Finally, to notify all of the event listeners of an event, you can use the `notify` method. If you recall, we used the `on` method in *Chapter 2, The Project Structure*, for our new settings page, like this: `backButton.on("tap", function (evt) { ... });`. In addition, the Declarative UI XML `<Button tap="tapAction" />` that we looked at earlier in this chapter attaches each of its events using the exact same Observable methods behind the scenes.

In NativeScript, you can attach multiple listeners to each event, and each one will be called when the event occurs. There is currently no way to cancel or stop the propagation of an event, so in NativeScript, all the event handlers will be called.

Binding

Binding is what allows us to do `<Edit value="{{ message }}">` in the Declarative UI and have it automatically update the edit value when the message value changes. The Bindable component handles all the binding and the callbacks for any bindable properties.

Using binding is actually simple. You need a source object, in this case, the message variable. You need the component itself, so again, in this example, the Edit component. Then, you just use the `bind` method on the Edit component to bind the source object to itself. Likewise, if you need to unbind, you would use the method named `unbind`.

The final property of the Bindable component is `bindingContext`, which is used to set the primary `Observable` object of the component and its children. If you recall in the prior chapter, the `main-page.js` file executed `page.bindingContext = vmModule.mainViewModel`. This code sets the page's `bindingContext` to the `Observable` object the `mainViewModel` file exported. This is needed so that the two bindings that are in the `main-page.xml` will connect to the source object. `{{ message }}` binds to the `mainViewModel.message` variable, and `{{ tapAction }}` binds to the `mainViewModel.tapAction` method.

Binding actually supports advanced features like ternary operators `{{ someVar === 'hello' ? "Hi" : someVar }}`, or expressions like `{{ someVar, "This is a " + someVar + ", neeto! " }}`, where it can do evaluations and show other values based on the result. The whole list of expressions can be viewed at `http://docs.nativescript.org/bindings.html#supported-expressions`.

Now that we have a much better grasp of the events and bindings, how about we switch gears and learn about how to apply a theme to your application and make it look any way you want it to be?

Styling the UI

The primary method to style our applications is the NativeScript variation on **Cascading Style Sheets** (**CSS**). If you are familiar with developing on a browser, then you should be right at home in NativeScript. If not, we will be walking you through a couple of examples to show how CSS works.

The NativeScript CSS has some differences from the normal CSS, but overall, it works pretty similar to how a browser does. How about we get started and discuss the what, why, how, and which of CSS. What is CSS, why use it, how is CSS applied, and finally, which properties does NativeScript currently support? Then, we will finish by looking at the main application wide `app.css` file to see how it is applied to our application.

What is CSS?

CSS is a styling language designed to allow you to create the presentation rules for a marked up file. In plain English, it allows you to separate your styles (that is, colors, sizes, positioning) from your markup (that is, the Declarative UI elements like Page and Button).

CSS is designed to allow later rules to cascade throughout and enhance or override prior rules. When I create a rule in my application-wide CSS file that all buttons need to be 40 point font, every single button in the application would then contain 40-point font. However, if in my `someOtherPage.css` file I put that all buttons on this page are supposed to be 20-point font, then the buttons on just this specific page would be 20-point. The rest of the buttons on every other page in my application would still be 40-point.

CSS is designed to allow more specific rules to override less specific rules. When I apply a general rule saying all buttons should be 40-point font, then I create another rule in the application-wide CSS saying all buttons that have the class of `Small` are to be 20-point. On the screen, you will see that any button without the `Small` `cssClass` would be 40-point, and those buttons that have the `Small` `cssClass` would be 20-point.

Why use CSS?

CSS allows you to easily create your own style for all the components throughout your application. Later in the application lifetime, if you decide or need to change your color scheme to match Apple or Google's newest color scheme, then all you need to do is change your CSS. It will then style all your pages without you having to touch every single component in your application. The other awesome thing about CSS is that you can have multiple application themes (like Light and Dark themes); all you need to do is apply the correct CSS file in one place and everything in your application is automatically updated.

How to use CSS

To set a value on a component (like size or color), we use something called a selector. A selector allows the CSS parser to figure out which component(s) each rule applies to. In a browser, there are a huge number of selectors and selector modifiers. NativeScript only supports the main three types of basic selectors, and you have no modifiers. The three selector types are ID, Class, and the Element or Component type. **ID** is the highest priority selector. The class, or `cssClass`, is the next highest priority. Finally, the element type is the lowest. The ID rule, `#myIdRule`, uses the ID you assign to the `id` property of the component and is prefixed with the pound (`#`) symbol.

A **class** rule looks like `.myClassName`; it is the class name you assign to a class or `cssClass` and is prefixed with a period symbol.

> In NativeScript v1.4, they finally added some logic to allow the XML class to be mapped to `cssClass`. So, throughout the book, you will see almost all the examples using `cssClass`, as `cssClass` has been the default since NativeScript was in the beginning stages; however, class is now the same valid property.

The **element** rule is just the name of the element or component; like Button or Label. CSS selectors are case-sensitive, so Button, button, buTTon or BUTTON all work the same.

Shall we check out a couple of sample rules? Here are five sample rules:

```
.MyClass { color: red; font-weight: bold; }
#MyId { color: green; }
Button { color: blue; }
Label { font-size: 10; }
StackLayout { font-size: 20; }
```

With these five rules, you might have guessed that `StackLayout` would be assigned a 20-point font. Whoa, wait a minute! `StackLayout` does not have any text; it is a layout. Why would I assign `StackLayout` a font size of 20? Well, the first word of CSS is **Cascading**. All components inside `StackLayout` will now get the default font size of 20 because of the values cascading.

Next, you will see that all Buttons normally start with blue text (with 20-point font). All Labels will be 10-point font, because the Label rule overrides the `StackLayout` rule. Now, for a bit more specificity, any component that had a class or `cssClass` equal to `MyClass` would get the color of red, and the text would be bolded. Any component that had an ID of `MyId` would finally become green.

So, if I had this: `<StackLayout><Button id="MyId" cssClass="MyClass"></StackLayout>`. what color would the button be? Would it be bold? What font size? The answers are: green, bold, and 20-point font. `StackLayout` would apply the 20-point font, `MyClass` would apply color and bolding, but `MyId` would then overwrite the `MyClass` color and apply its color since ID rules are the highest priority rules.

Configuring your CSS Rules

Just like with a browser, the following or later CSS rules override the preceding rules. So, if my CSS was:

```
#Awesome { font-size: 20; color: green; }
... other css rules ...
#Awesome { font-size: 22; }
```

Anything that was using the ID of `Awesome` would be green (first rule) but would have the font size of 22 applied, since the last rule overrode the first rule.

In NativeScript, there are several places you can put your CSS rules, including the application-wide `app.css` file, which we mentioned earlier and is configured via the `app.js` file. Anything you want applied or accessible from all pages is put in the `app.css` file. This application-wide CSS file is applied first. Then, the `pageName.css` file is applied; this file is only used on that single page named exactly like it. Then, in JavaScript, you can call `Page.addCssFile()` to apply any additional files, or you can call `Page.addCss()` to append a CSS string to the page. These two commands are applied in the order that the statements run.

The Page component also has a `.css` property. You can read it to see all the CSS rules that are currently applied to the page. However, if you assign anything to it, it will clear all CSS already applied to the page except the application-wide CSS. So, if all you are wanting to do is append some more CSS to the page, make sure you use the `Page.addCss()` method, not the `.css` property.

Finally, each component has its own `.style` property. The `.style` property has multiple subproperties, which are what control the look and feel of that component. All CSS ultimately gets applied to the actual component style. A small note of discrepancy: in the Declarative UI, you can execute `<Label style="padding-left:2; padding-right:2">;` however, in JavaScript, you have to execute `Label.style.paddingLeft = 2;` You cannot execute `Label.style="padding-left:2";` because when the Declarative UI goes to apply the style string property, it automatically parses it into the subproperties and then applies each of the subproperties.

In CSS, all styles are in the format of name-name (name dash name called kebab-case) instead of a space, for example, `background-color` or `padding-top`. CSS properties are case-sensitive in NativeScript. In JavaScript, the dash is removed and then the following letter is capitalized. The name ends up being camel-cased, like `.backgroundColor` or `.paddingTop`.

Existing CSS properties

Now, here is where a major difference occurs between NativeScript and browsers. The number of properties is completely different. Most browsers support over 300 standardized CSS properties, and many more browser-specific CSS properties. Since a browser is designed to render markup in different ways, it needs help to be precise so it has a huge number of CSS properties. In NativeScript, you build things totally differently, and so it currently only has around 30 CSS properties. Let us discuss how and which properties work.

CSS property	**JavaScript property**	**Description and supported value**
`background-color`	`backgroundColor`	Sets the background color. Supports `Color*`.
`background-image`	`backgroundImage`	Sets the background image. Supports `String` (path or resource).
`background-position`	`backgroundPosition`	Sets the background image position. Supports `Absolute`, `Positioning`, or `Percentage`.
`background-repeat`	`backgroundRepeat`	Sets the background image repeatability. Supports `repeat`, `repeat-x`, `repeat-y`, and `no-repeat`.
`background-size`	`backgroundSize`	Sets the background image size. Supports "`height#, width#`", "`height%, width%`", "`cover`", or "`contain`".
`border-color`	`borderColor`	Sets the border color. Supports `Color*`.
`border-radius`	`borderRadius`	Sets the border radius. Supports `Integer`.
`border-width`	`borderWidth`	Sets a border width. Supports `Integer`.
`color`	`color`	Sets the foreground or text color. Supports `Color*`.
`font`	`font`	Sets the font properties; the format should be: `font-family`, `font-size`, `font-style`, and `font-weight`. Example: "`Arial, Times 12 Bold`".

CSS property	JavaScript property	Description and supported value
font-family	fontFamily	Sets the font family. Example: Arial, Times, Serif.
font-size	fontSize	Sets the font size. Supports Integer.
font-style	fontStyle	Sets the font style. Supports italic or normal.
font-weight	fontWeight	Sets the font weight. Supports bold or normal.
height	height	Sets the height. Supports Integer.
horizontal-align	horizontalAlignment	Sets the horizontal alignment. Supports left, center, right, or stretch.
margin	margin	Sets the margin sides. Supports Integer.
margin-bottom	marginBottom	Sets the bottom margin. Supports Integer.
margin-left	marginLeft	Sets the left margin. Supports Integer.
margin-right	marginRight	Sets the right margin. Supports Integer.
margin-top	marginTop	Sets the top margin. Supports Integer.
min-height	minHeight	Sets the minimal height. Supports Integer.
min-width	minWidth	Sets the minimal width. Supports Integer.
opacity	opacity	Sets the opacity. Supports decimals from 0.0 (fully transparent) to 1.0 (fully opaque).
padding	padding	Padding for layout sides. Supports Integer.
padding-bottom	paddingBottom	Padding for layout bottom. Supports Integer.
padding-left	paddingLeft	Padding for layout left. Supports Integer.
padding-right	paddingRight	Padding for layout right. Supports Integer.

CSS property	JavaScript property	Description and supported value
padding-top	paddingTop	Padding for layout top. Supports Integer.
text-align	textAlignment	Sets text alignment. Supports left, center, or right.
vertical-align	verticalAlignment	Sets the vertical alignment. Supports top, center, bottom, or stretch.
visibility	visibility	Sets the visibility. Supports visible or collapse.
width	width	Sets the width. Supports Integer.

* Color Support is very thorough in NativeScript. Colors can be named Blue, Aquamarine, and Pink, for example. They can also be Alpha, Red, Green, and Blue hexadecimal in the following standard formats: #RGB, #RRGGBB, or #AARRGGBB.

As you can see, there are a large number of standard properties that apply to almost all components. Padding is one of the few properties that I will point out only supports a couple of the components. Otherwise, virtually all the visual components support each of these CSS properties. The other difference that should be noted is that concerning all size and location property values, where in a browser you might use em, px, or %, NativeScript does not currently support any of these; you just use the raw device independent pixel number with no number qualifier. In future versions of NativeScript the % may be supported.

Exploring app.css

We glossed over this file earlier in the chapter, so how about we finally dissect it and see how it styles our application? The `app.css` file that comes in our awesome application looks like this:

```
.title {
  font-size: 30;
  horizontal-align: center;
  margin:20;
}
```

```
Button {
  font-size: 42;
  horizontal-align: center;
}

.message {
  font-size: 20;
  color: #284848;
  horizontal-align: center;
}
```

Well, this file is simple now that we understand the CSS rules and properties. The first rule (`.title`) is a class rule (because it uses the period in it). Any component that has the `cssClass` of `title` will have the rule applied to it, which is:

- Font size of 30
- Center-aligned
- Margin of 20 (DP) device independent pixels all around it

In our `main-page.xml` file, that component is a first label and it says **Tap the button**. The second rule (`Button`) is an element or component rule (because it is the name of a component). Any component that is a button will have the rule applied to it, which is:

- Font size of 42
- Center-aligned

This rule matches both the button on the main page and our new button in the settings file. This is why the **Go Back** button on the settings page was so large. The third rule is another class rule (`.message`); any component that has the `cssClass` of `message` will have its rule applied to it, which is:

- Font size of 20
- Colored a greyish color
- Center-aligned

This is used by the second label, which says **42 taps left**. This is also the same `cssClass` that we choose to use in our new settings file.

Trying CSS out and styling our application

Let us open up our `app.css` file and make some changes. First of all, I really want a white background rather than gray. Can you guess which selector and CSS property we need to use? Your best bet is to use the Page selector; however, `StackLayout` would work in the current case because it also covers the entire page. The property is `background-color`.

Next, I would like the **Tap the button** message to stand out a bit more. So, let us do a couple of things. We need to modify the `.title` rule and reduce the margin to 10. To make the font stand out a bit more, how about we bold it and change the color to #FF0111?

Next, we really want the button to stand out. So, we will change the Button rules. First off, I like rounded corners. We need to add a border-radius of 15 to it. Since we added a radius, we need to actually define the background color to be `#dddddd`. We also need to tell it how wide we want the button to be to make it look sharp. I am choosing a width of 150. Finally, we will change the font size to 50.

Man, we can't forget about the message rule; so how about we add a margin-top of 10 and then change the font color to `#3ca8dd`? Our final `app.css` file should look like this:

```
Page {
  background-color: white;
}

.title {
  font-size: 30;
  horizontal-align: center;
  margin: 10;
  font-weight: bold;
  color: #FF0111;
}

button {
  font-size: 50;
  horizontal-align: center;
  border-radius: 15;
  width: 150;
  background-color: #dddddd;
}
```

```
.message {
  margin-top: 10;
  font-size: 20;
  color: #3ca8dd;
  horizontal-align: center;
}
```

Now, go ahead, and execute a `nativescript run android --emulator` command and check out the results, which look like this:

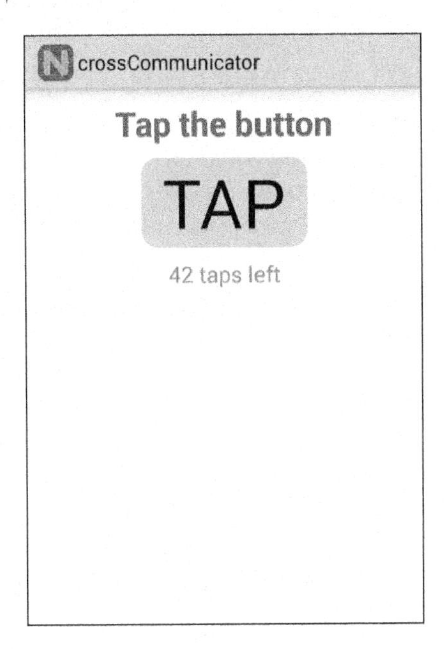

Styling on your own

I would recommend you take a few minutes to play around and try styling the application via the `app.css` file. Try going into the settings screen; do you notice how the settings button is now not very nice-looking? Well, see if you can fix it without messing up the main screen. Try and change your background, fonts, margins, and padding. You can then create a new `settings.css` or a `main-page.css` file to play with styling for just one page. See how your local `page.css` files override the `app.css` file rules. Can you create rules that style multiple labels one way, but then create a more specific rule that overrides only part of the rules for some of them? Please feel free to modify any of your application files. Your imagination is the limit.

Summary

We covered a lot in this chapter. You learned how the Declarative UI works, from the XML parser and how it parses to how to develop your screens in Declarative UI. You also learned which component handles all the events in the system. In addition, you learned how visual components, by being a descendant in the view tree, all have access to a large number of properties, events, and methods. Then, we learned how NativeScript styles your pages and components. Next, we learned how to use the CSS to style a single item on a single page to every item on all pages in our application. Finally, we made our application stand out a lot more by styling the main items.

Now that you have a solid understanding on how the entire system works, we are going to change the sample application into a real communication application in the next chapter. We are going to dig into lots of code, CSS, and Declarative UI. We will also get to look at several new visual components and finally use several non-visual components.

4
Building a Featured Application

Awesome! We have finally made it to the point where we can start getting into the meat of the application. We have covered a lot in the earlier chapters. So, hold on tight as we actually finally get to build a fully functional NativeScript cross-device communication application.

In this chapter, we will cover the following topics:

- Layouts
- Building our featured application
- Nonvisual components
- Building the main screen
- Fonts
- Icons
- Communication with the server
- Trying out our application

Layouts

I will cover the different `Layout` types that NativeScript offers. We have already covered StackLayout in the previous chapters. To keep things in one place for your easy reference, I will briefly cover StackeLayout again. In addition to the descriptions here, the Layouter program, containing a sample of each of these layouts, is included with this book or can be downloaded from `https://github.com/GettingStartedWithNativeScript`.

StackLayout

The StackLayout allows you to stack things either vertically or horizontally. It will only put a single item into each layout slot. The layout slot will be either the entire width of the screen or the full height of the screen. Each item can use as much height or width in the stacking direction. For example in horizontal layout, black needed way less room than light black. In the vertical layout, you can see shade 2 uses more height than shade 1. To choose the horizontal version, you need to set the orientation= "horizontal". By default, it will be vertical. Look at the following sample:

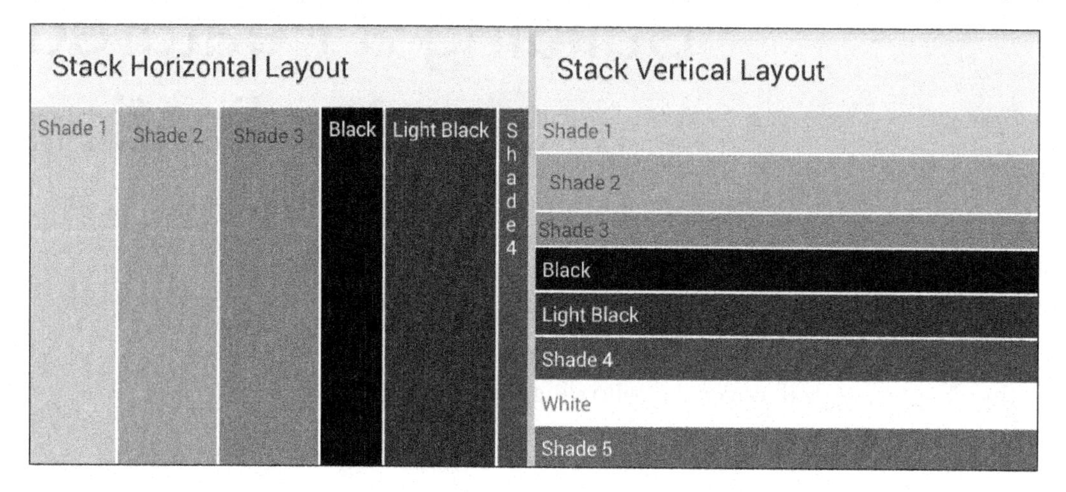

WrapLayout

This layout, as you would expect from its name, will keep putting items next to each other on the same line until it has to wrap them. The height of each line will be the same. So, all items on the line will take the amount of physical height space on the line, leaving you with a blank area around any items that are not as tall. As you can see from the preceding sample, shade 1 is not as tall as shade 2, and even though there is a lot of room, shade 3 does not automatically move up and fit into that space. Each whole line still takes the same height as its tallest item. The other thing is that shade 3 is set to wrap words internally, but the wrap layout does not wrap words. The whole label is wrapped to the next line, as shown here:

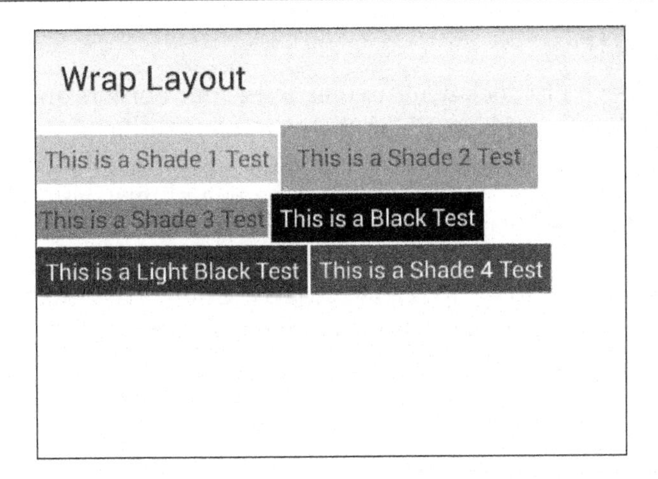

AbsoluteLayout

AbsoluteLayout is, well, absolute. Funny, I know—I should have been a comedian. In AbsoluteLayout, you give each child a position in the top-left corner of the screen. The components will then layout in the order that they are declared. In this image, you can see that shade 3 was declared earlier in the component order, and shade 4 was declared later, as it overlaps shade 3 and shade 2:

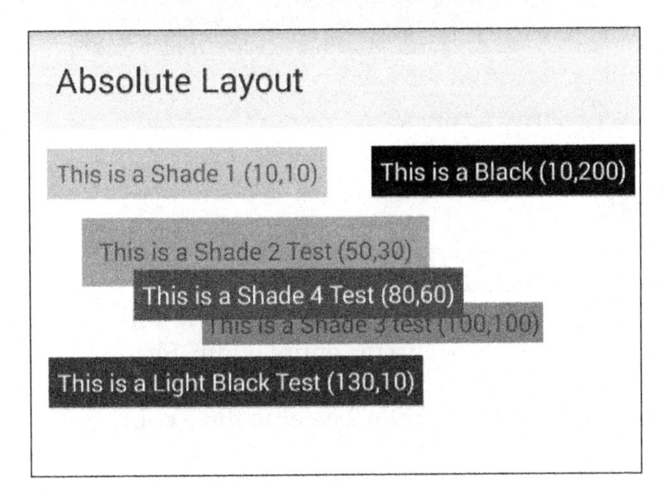

DockLayout

DockLayout allows you to dock items to one of the four borders and/or fill the screen with the last declared item. So, in this example, I declared the first item on the bottom, then to the left, then to the top, then to the right, and then, finally, at the center. You only have to declare the sides you want, and then, you can choose to fill the remainder of the screen with the final declared child in the dock layout. To choose the site, you can set `dock="SIDE"` on the child element, or in the declaration of DockLayout, you can add `stretchLastChild="true"` to cause the very last child to fill up the remaining space. Look at the following screenshot:

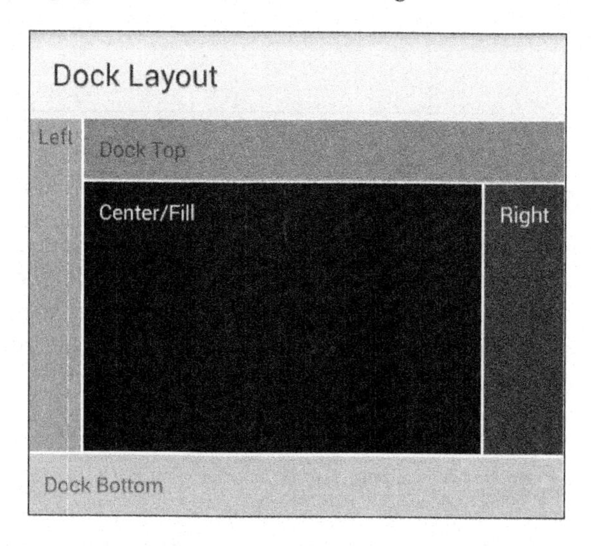

GridLayout

The final layout I am describing is probably the most awesome of the bunch. The image does not do it justice. In the first image, I declared a 4 × 4 grid. I made it have four equal columns and four auto-sized rows. The shade 1 item is set to have a colspan of four columns, so it takes up the entire width. Shade 3 is set to only take one column, so it wraps onto the next line. Black, light black, and shade 4 are all set to take two columns each. Finally, shade 2 is set to three columns, as shown in this image:

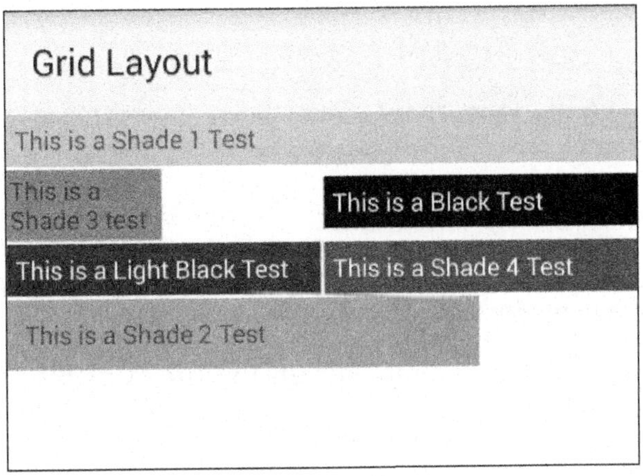

Grid Layout

This is a Shade 1 Test

This is a Shade 3 test

This is a Black Test

This is a Light Black Test

This is a Shade 4 Test

This is a Shade 2 Test

	Column 0	Column 1	Column 2	....	Column X
Row 0					
Row 1					
Row 2					
...					
Row Y					

To make sure you understand a column and row layout, this image shows you how columns and rows are laid out. NativeScript starts with **Column0** and **Row0**. Each item in the grid item can span one to multiple columns and/or one to multiple rows. Each column and/or row can also be a different height from any other row or column. On `GridLayout` itself, you need to declare `columns= "x,x,x..."` and `rows= "x,x,x..."`, where `x` can be a star, a number, or an auto size. On the child elements, you need to tell them which row and column they are in and whether they have a `rowSpan` or `colSpan` value. We will discuss `GridLayouts` and the star, number, and auto sizes later in this chapter with real examples.

Currently, these are the built-in layouts in NativeScript. With these layouts, you can pretty much build any screen you want. You can easily mix and match layouts by putting layouts within layouts. You can nest any layout inside another layout.

Here is an example:

```
<StackLayout>
<StackLayout orientation="horizontal"> ... </StackLayout>
<StackLayout orientation="horizontal"> ... </StackLayout>
...
</StackLayout>
```

You can easily add a `StackLayout` property inside a `StackLayout` property to allow you to have multiple items in each vertical row.

Now that we have seen all the different layouts that are available, let's work on building our application.

Building our featured application

We will now build a full-featured cross-platform communication application. This application will ultimately allow you to have real-time communication with any other people connected to the same server. The application will run the exact same way on each of the platforms. By the time we are done, the application will look like this:

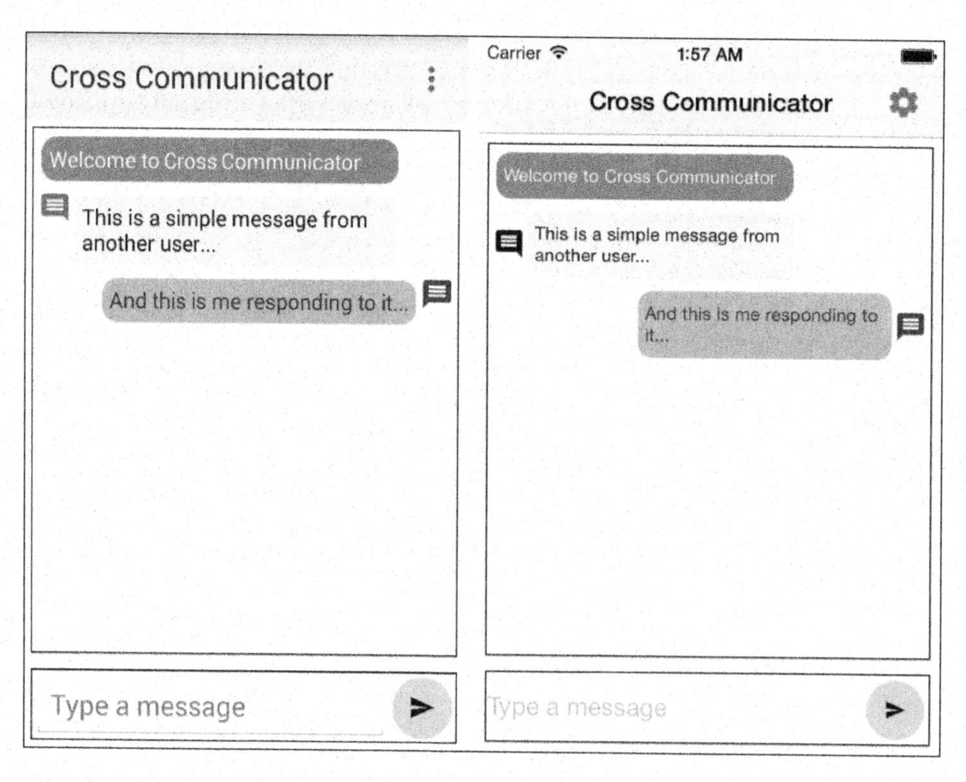

The first thing we will work on is the settings screen, as we need some place to put in the server address and your name. Then, we will begin work on the main application screen. Let's get this show on the road!

Nonvisual components

In the prior chapters, we started to create a page called **settings**, but now, we actually need to convert it from that simple demo test screen into a real settings screen. For this screen to work properly, we need a component that we can use to store information when our application is no longer running. The best component for this is the **application-settings** component. This is a nonvisual component, meaning you do not create it in the Declarative UI XML. This is constructed and used in JavaScript. This component has only a couple of simple methods, but the most important thing is that the settings are persistent so that we can access them forever.

So, let's open up our `settings.js` file and completely empty it. We will totally rewrite it, and I shall show you how we will use this awesome component. The first change we will make is to require the `application-settings` module. So, your code should start like this:

```
var appSettings = require('application-settings');
var Observable = require("data/observable").Observable;
var dialogs = require('ui/dialogs');
```

As you can see, we are loading the `application-settings`, `observable` and `dialog` components. The `application-settings` component does the persisting of data. We covered the `Observable` component in *Chapter 3, Declarative UI, Styling, and Events*. Finally, the `dialog` component allows you to create dialogs easily, and you will see how we use it at the end of the `settings.js` code.

The next step is to set up our page-wide variables. This is simple. We just want to store the actual `page` variable, and we need to create an `observable` variable with `name` and `server` values, as these are the two settings that we will persist. The code will look like this:

```
var page;
var settings = new Observable();
settings.set("name","Guest");
settings.set("server","nativescript.rocks:3000");
```

That was simple! We just defined two variables and set two properties on the observable. The next part of the code is the actual functions that do the work on the screen. The first function that we need will be very similar to the code we explored in earlier chapters. We need to capture and assign the `page` variable, and we need to set the binding up. The best event to do this in is the `loaded` event:

```
exports.loaded = function(args) {
  page = args.object;
  page.bindingContext = settings;
};
```

Simple enough, assign the `page` variable and set the `page.bindingContext` variable to our setting observable variable we just declared.

Now comes the fun part. We need to retrieve our stored settings. We could have done it in the `loaded` event, but this event only fires the very first time the page is created. We actually want to load the values each time we show the settings page. To accomplish this, we will use the `shownModally` event function like this:

```
exports.shownModally=function() {
  if (appSettings.getBoolean("setup")) {
    settings.set("name", appSettings.getString("name"));
    settings.set("server", appSettings.getString("server"));
  }
};
```

If you have not guessed how this works, it is straightforward. We are checking to see whether we have ever saved it before. If we have saved it before, then we would load the `name` and `server` variables from our persistent storage and then set them on the `settings` observable variable. Let's see whether you can guess the next piece of the puzzle since we just loaded the values. Yes, you got it—we need to save the values. So, being totally original, I named it, as shown here:

```
exports.save = function() {
  if (!checkFieldValue('name')) return;
  if (!checkFieldValue('server')) return;

  appSettings.setBoolean("setup", true);
  appSettings.setString("name", settings.get('name'));
  appSettings.setString("server", settings.get('server'));
  page.closeModal();
};
```

OK. So, that was not nearly as original as I claimed, but what else would you name it? The `save()` function runs a function to verify that the `name` and `server` values are not blank before it saves the data. Then, it saves the data and closes the dialog.

Following the `save` routine, we want a visible way to cancel the dialog. Can you guess the next function name? Let's take a look at the following code snippet:

```
exports.cancel = function() {
  page.closeModal();
};
```

Wow, that was some seriously complicated code, right? Oh, wait! I am thinking of some other function. In this very simple function, all we do is close the dialog. This is part of the reason we want to reload the values each time we open up the settings page. We want to make sure when you reopen the settings, it has the current settings and not the last changed values that you just cancelled. Note that on the Android, you can also cancel the page by touching anywhere outside the page. This is the second part of the reason I chose to load the values at opening. The final and the best reason is we only have to have the load or reset code in one place to handle all the cases.

The final function that we have is the `checkFieldValue()` function, which I called in the `save` routine. It is used to make the end users have a little cleaner experience when they do not put in the values we expect. So, here it is:

```
function checkFieldValue(field) {
  var fieldValue = settings.get(field);
  if (!fieldValue) {
    dialogs.alert("The "+field+" can't be left blank.  Please fill
    in a value.");
    var fieldId = page.getViewById(field);
    if (fieldId) {
      fieldId.focus();
    }
    return false;
  }
  return true;
}
```

This function is straightforward. First, we retrieved the value from the observable, and if it is blank, then we show an error dialog. Finally, we attempted to find the field for this value on the screen and refocus on that specific field. Let's expand a bit on the dialogs.

Dialogs

NativeScript has several built-in dialogs, but the dialogs in NativeScript are actually quite different than what you may be used to—they do not block execution. They are totally asynchronous. Take a look at the following lines of code:

```
console.log("Hi I'm before dialog");
dialogs.alert("Hey").then(function() {
  console.log("Dialog done");
});
console.log("Hi I'm after the dialog");
```

It will print the following output:

```
Hi I'm before dialog
Hi I'm after the dialog
Dialog done
```

Your code continues running even though a dialog is up. The `then()` function sets the callback code that will run when you close the dialog. All the dialogs use the ES6 promises-based system, which we will explore now.

ES6 is the standard for the next version of JavaScript. It actually stands for ECMAScript 6. The ECMA standards body produces new standards where JavaScript is the implementation of the language from the standards group.

Before we diverge again, let's finish looking at the different types of dialogs available. Then, we will explore promises. The object you pass into the dialog routines is typically an object that can or will contain one or more of these:

```
{
  title: "The Title of the Dialog",
  message: "The Message in the Dialog",
  okButtonText: "The Ok Button Text",
  cancelButtonText: "The Cancel Button Text",
  defaultText: "The default prompt text",
  username: "Default User Name",
  password: "Default Password",
  actions: ["An", "Array", "Of", "Actions"]
}
```

Alert dialog

You have the standard Alert dialog, which allows you to set a message and a title, and has a **OK** button. You can call it using `dialogs.alert({title: "My Alert Title", message: "My Message", okButtonText: "Click me!"}).then(…);`. It looks like this:

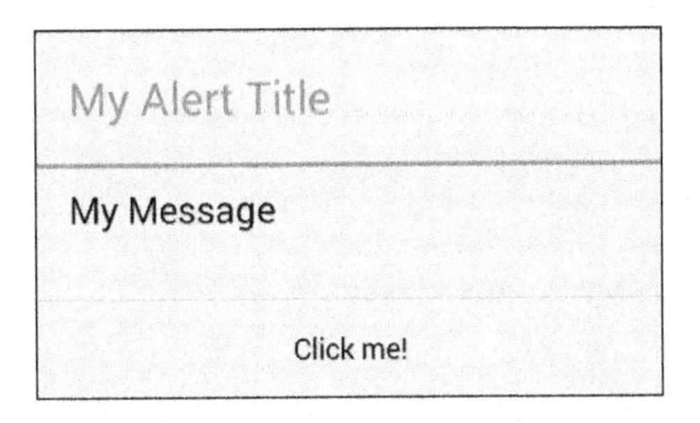

Confirm dialog

This dialog allows you to ask a yes/ok or no/cancel type question. You can also change the title, message, and both buttons' text, as shown in the following screenshot. This one is called via `dialogs.confirm({title: "My Confirm Title", message: "My Message", okButtonText: "Ok Button!", cancelButtonText: "Cancel Me"}).then(…);`:

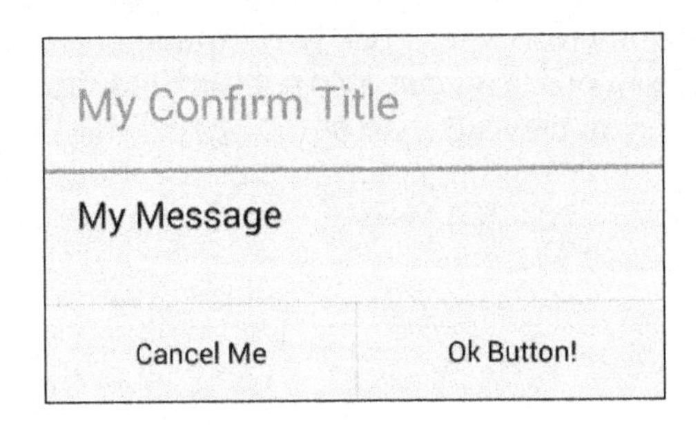

Prompt dialog

This dialog allows you to ask for an answer. You can also set the same title, header, button, and even the input type and default value (see the following image). You call this one using `dialogs.prompt({title: "My Prompt Title", message: "My Prompt Message", defaultText: "Default Text", okButtonText: "Ok Button!", cancelButtonText: "Cancel Me"});`. Look at the following screenshot:

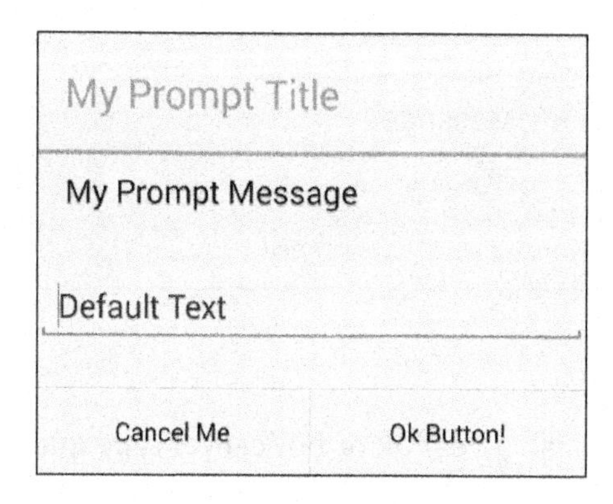

Login dialog

This dialog also has the ability to change the title, message, and buttons, as shown in the following screenshot. However, it has two inputs: one of them for a username and one of them for a password. You can also set the defaults for both of them. To open up the login dialog, you can call `dialogs.login({userName: "Username", password: "password", title: "My Login Title", message: "My Login Message", okButtonText: "Ok Button!", cancelButtonText: "Cancel Me"}).then(...);`.

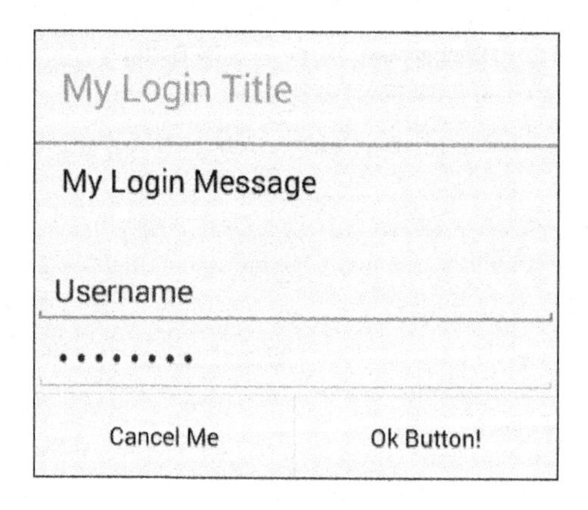

Action dialog

This dialog gives you a list of items you can choose. When the item gets chosen, it returns a value. It also allows you to change the title, message, and button texts (see the following image). To open the action dialog, you can call `dialogs.action({title: "My Action Title", message: "My Action Message", cancelButtonText: "Cancel Me", actions: ["Apple", "Orange", "Grape"]}).then(...);`.

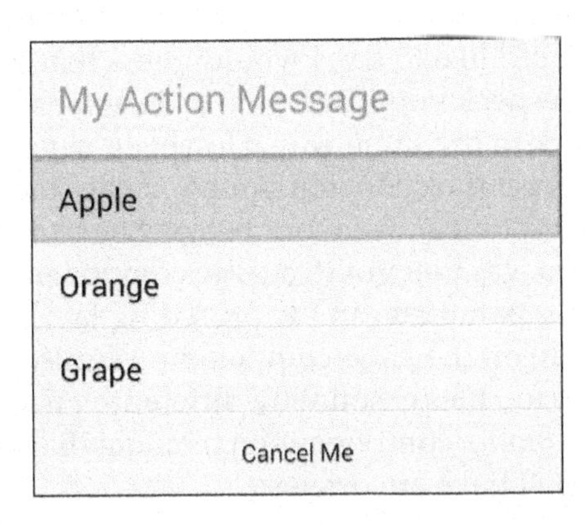

You can also explore these dialogs and the code to generate them in the layouter program, which can be downloaded from `https://github.com/GettingStartedWithNativeScript`. Now, let's take a look at what promises are, which is what dialog, and what many other NativeScript components returns.

Promises

NativeScript in a lot of its code actually uses the newer ES6 promise-based standard system. Instead of passing a callback into the function, the code returns a promise object on which you can use a `then()` or `catch()` function. The `then()` function allows you to set up your function you want to run when the promise is successful. The `catch()` function is what allows you to set up a function to be run when the promise has failed. An example would look like this:

```
var processCompleted = doSomeAsyncTask();
processCompleted.then(handleSuccess).catch(handleError);
```

You can chain the `then()` and `catch()` functions, or you can call the `processCompleted` parameter separately with a `then()` function and then, add a `catch()` function later. You can also chain promises so that the results of one promise are returned as another promise. Mozilla has an overview of ES6 promises at `https://developer.mozilla.org/en-US/docs/Web/JavaScript/Reference/Global_Objects/Promise`.

So, now that we checked out dialogs and promises, let's resume working on the application and work on the Declarative UI for this settings screen.

The settings screen Declarative UI

The Declarative UI code is actually compact. So, let's open up the `settings.xml` file. We are simply creating a page with two text entry fields and two buttons. Based on the actual preceding code, you can probably even write the majority, if not all of the UI, yourself. If you would like to try, I would guess that once you are done with this little exercise, you can check your awesome code against mine. Functionally, I would expect them to work in the same way. However, since I will use this screen to describe a new layout type, the code will not be exactly the same, as I will be cheating and using this awesome new layout before I have explained it to you. So, the first item on the page is, yes you got it, a `Page` component. So, if you remember, we used the `shownModally` parameter in the preceding JavaScript and loaded events. We are assigning them here on the `Page` component. We also want to set `Page.actionBarHidden` to be `true`, the reason why different versions of NativeScript have fixed and broken the `actionBar` component on a modal dialog. So, we are just going to disable it so that we won't have any issues:

```
<Page shownModally="shownModally" loaded="loaded"
actionBarHidden="true">
```

That was simple, and I would guess our code should be similar at this point. Now, here is where our files probably diverge. You probably used the `StackLayout` component as that is the only layout we have covered so far in the last three chapters. How about covering the awesome `GridLayout`?

GridLayouts

Now, I will show you the true power of the dark side, `GridLayout`. Take a look at the following code:

```
<GridLayout columns="*,*,*,*" rows="auto,auto,auto,auto"
cssClass="border">
```

Whoa, what in the world is that? Gibberish? That just plainly looks scary. So, my first question, what does the asterisk mean? And for the second question, what is auto? What? You cannot answer those two simple questions? Well, I don't blame you. I will give you a minute to go read the docs about what those are for. Oh, all right, I will explain them to you. There goes my awesomely competitive edge as I explain the arcane parameters of GridLayout.

In the preceding `GridLayout` declaration, I am declaring four columns. Those four asterisks mean that we should split up the remaining column space equally. In this case, each column is getting 1/4th of the screen width. On a screen that was 600 pixels wide, each column would get 150 pixels. Now, the rows, which I set to auto, mean that each of the four rows will get exactly the required height that the components in that row needs. In both the columns and rows definitions, I can use an asterisk (*), an auto, or a pixel number. You can also even mix and match all of them, if I use `100,*,auto,auto,*` it would render it as: column 0=100 device independent pixels. Column 2 and 3 get the width of the largest component that is defined inside its own column. Finally column 1 and 4 each get half the remaining size.

There is one more advanced technique with the asterisk. You can actually specify something like `*,2*,*`, which means that the center column gets two equal widths for its size. So, on a 600-pixel screen, it would be like you put `150,300,150` for the values. Now, the next piece would be how we assign the components to each row and column. Here is the rest of the Declarative UI code:

```
<Label row="0" colSpan="4" text="Settings" cssClass="title" />
<Label row="1" text="Name: " /><TextField id="name" col="1"
colSpan="3" row="1" hint="Enter your name" text="{{name}}" />
<Label row="2" text="Server: " /><TextField id="server" col="1"
colSpan="3" row="2" hint="Enter a server" text="{{server}}"/>

<Button row="3" col="0" colSpan="2" text="Save" tap="save" />
<Button row="3" col="2" colSpan="2" text="Cancel" tap="cancel" />
</GridLayout></Page>
```

As you can see, in each of the components, we are declaring a `col`, `row`, and sometimes, a `colSpan` value. If I did not declare a `row` or `col` field, then they, by default, would be zero. To help visualize this, I created the same settings screen so that it would have a light blue color for every other column:

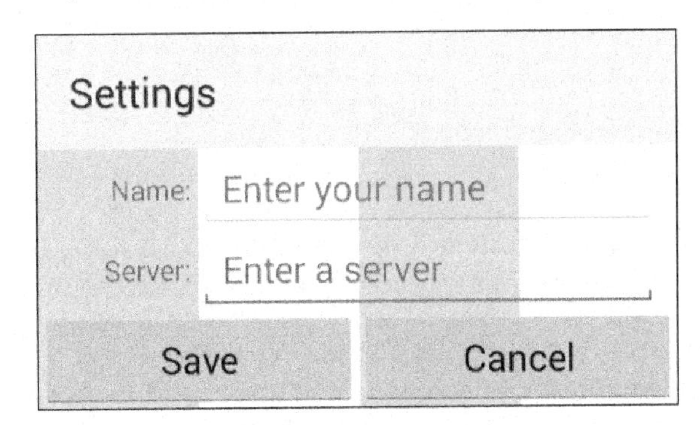

You can see from this screenshot that the **Name** label is in column zero. `TextField` is in column one and has a column span of three. The **Server** label is in column zero, row two. Again, `TextField` has column one and a column span of three. The buttons are in row three, and each has a column span of two. Using `GridLayout`, I am able to layout the dialog box in a clear and clean interface for our users. The reason I chose to divide the screen into four columns was that I had two buttons. I needed to make each of them take up half the screen, which meant I needed a number I could divide by two.

Now, if you get antsy and decide to run the settings screen right now, it won't exactly look like that. Why? Well, you don't have any of the CSS to make everything align nicely. Here is the simple CSS:

```
Label {
  padding: 2; vertical-align: center; horizontal-align: right;
}

.border {
  border-color: black;     background-color: white;
  margin: 0;
}

.title {
  background-color: gainsboro;
  font-size:26;      font-weight: bold;
  padding: 4;        padding-left: 10;
  horizontal-align: stretch;
}

TextField {
  margin-right: 10;
}

Button {
  padding: 2;
}
```

I added some simple padding, font styling, and margin on some of the layout items to make it look nicer. It is pretty simple to adjust and make the interface look a bit sharper.

Now, let's dig into the actual main screen of the application since we have finished creating the settings screen.

Building the main screen

We will start with the code of the application, as it is fairly simple and gives you some context for the rest of the screen. Then, we will dig into the screen Declarative UI and finish off with the CSS for the screen.

JavaScript code

The main screen code is straightforward. We need to require the same application settings as we used in the settings screen to see whether we need to make the settings screen pop up. Then, we will require the observable array, which holds all our messages. Then, we will include a file that deals with our communication, which we will discuss after the screen is done. Let's take a look at the following code snippet:

```
var appSettings = require('application-settings');
var ObservableArray = require("data/observable-
array").ObservableArray;
var Socket = require("./AjaxSocket.js").AJAXSocket;
```

Next, we will define the icon array and the message array. Each of the icon values, such as `0xE0C9`, is easily accessible on the icon fonts website. We will discuss more about the icon fonts later in this chapter when we discuss them in depth. Let's look at the following code snippet:

```
var messageIcons = ["", String.fromCharCode(0xE0C9),
String.fromCharCode(0xE85A), String.fromCharCode(0xE0B9)];
var messages = new ObservableArray();
messages.on('change', trackMessages);
messages.push({from: 0, message: "Welcome to Cross
Communicator"});

var socket = new Socket();
socket.on('message', function(evt) {
  newMessage({from: evt.from, message: evt.data});
});

var entry, scrollView, page;
```

We also want to track whether the message array is changed and run our own function (`trackMessage`) on it. Then, we will create an instance of our communication library and set it to call `newMessage` when a new message comes in. Then, we will create a couple of global variables to contain our `scrollview`, `page`, and text `entry` controls. All in all, the code is so far simple. Wow! We will need to work on the functions on the main screen. Let's start by exploring the `trackMessage()` function first:

```
var trackerCounter = null;
function trackMessages(evt) {
  if (evt && evt.action && evt.action !== "add") { return; }
  while (messages.length > 40) {
    messages.shift();
  }
  if (trackerCounter || !scrollView) { return; }
  trackerCounter = setTimeout(resetMessageDisplay,1);
}
```

As you can see, the `trackMessages` function checks to see whether it is an `add` event. Then, it checks the length of the message queue. We do not want to exceed the memory on some of the low-memory devices, so we only cache the last 40 messages. Any messages over 40 are discarded. Then, it checks to see whether the `resetMessageDisplay` routine is already scheduled to run, and if it isn't, it schedules it. Let's check out the `resetMessageDisplay` function next:

```
function resetMessageDisplay() {
  trackerCounter = null;
  var offset = scrollView.scrollableHeight;
  scrollView.scrollToVerticalOffset(offset, false);
}
```

As you can see from this, we basically cleared the `trackerCounter` variable. Then, we will find out how much scroll room the `scrollview` parameter has, and then we will move the `scrollView` parameter to the end of the display. We want to keep the display in sync to always show the bottom of a message when any new messages come in. The next function we will look at is the `pageLoaded` function:

```
exports.pageLoaded = function (args) {
  page = args.object;
  entry = page.getViewById("entry");
  scrollView = page.getViewById("scroller");
  page.bindingContext = { messages: messages };
}
```

This code is pretty simple. We grabbed and assigned the `page` variable. We used it to look up the `entry` and `scrollView` controls that are on the page and assigned them to our variables. Then, we set up the binding so that the `messages` variable is in the binding context. Now, because of a bug in iOS, we also have to define the `navigatedTo` event instead of just including this code in our `pageLoaded` event, so we will look at this one next:

```
exports.navigatedTo = function(args) {
  if (!page) { page = args.object; }
```

```
    showDialog();
    trackerCounter = setTimeout(resetMessageDisplay,1);
  };
```

In this function, all we do is set up our page variable if it hasn't been already set up and then call our `showDialog` routine. Then, we set up `resetMessageDisplay` to fire immediately after all the other code that has run. Our `showDialog()` function is next in line to be explored:

```
function showDialog(force) {
  if (!appSettings.getBoolean('setup', false) || force === true) {
    page.showModal('settings', '', function() {
      socket.setHost(appSettings.getString('server'));
      socket.setName(appSettings.getString('name'));
    }, false);
  }
  else {
    socket.setHost(appSettings.getString('server'));
    socket.setName(appSettings.getString('name'));
  }
}
```

Here is where we use the application settings to see whether we have already saved our settings. On a new install, we won't have the `setup` variable set, so the dialog will automatically show up when the application first runs. Once the dialog is done running or if the dialog is skipped, we will load the settings and apply them to the socket class. The next function is how we trigger the settings dialog manually:

```
exports.settingsTap = function() {
  showDialog(true);
};
```

In this case, we pass in `true` to force the dialog to open. Then, the final part of this is the message delivery. We need to be able to send and get messages to our server:

```
exports.goTap = function() {
  if (entry.text.length > 0) {
    var data = {from: 1, message: entry.text};
    entry.text = "";
    newMessage(data);
    sendMessage(data.message);
  }
};

function newMessage(msg) {
  if (msg.from < 3) {
```

```
      msg.iconLeft = messageIcons[msg.from];
    }
    else {
      Msg.iconRight = messageIcons[msg.from]
    }
    messages.push(msg);
  }

  function sendMessage(m) {
    socket.send(m);
  }
```

As you can see from the preceding code, it is simple. We basically are setting up our screen configuration and how the messages are handled. Now that we have finished all the code for the main screen, how about we check out the main screen Declarative UI XML?

Declarative UI

I will start this one in a away different from how I normally present a screen. We will look at the finished screen first, and then, you can see whether you can surmise the majority of the pieces I used and how I built the screen. Then, we will discuss each of the pieces as we build the screen. In this example, I cheated and put a couple more messages in the message queue to show how it will look when completed. On the left-hand side is Android, and on the right-hand side is iOS:

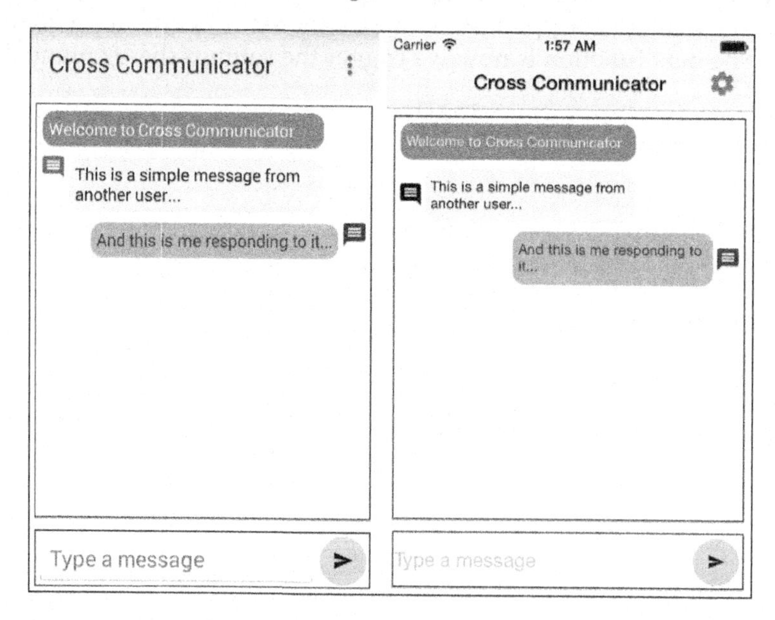

As you can see, both platforms look pretty much the same.

Main page Declarative UI

Well, let's first dig in to the Declarative UI. Now, the first part of the screen is just the standard definition. We have a `<Page>` declaration and then a `<ActionBar>` declaration. However, this is where we will learn about menus. Do you see that vertical ellipsis up there in the right-hand corner of the Android (left screen)? Well, on an Android device, this is a pop-down menu. You click on it, and it expands and shows you menu items, as in this screenshot:

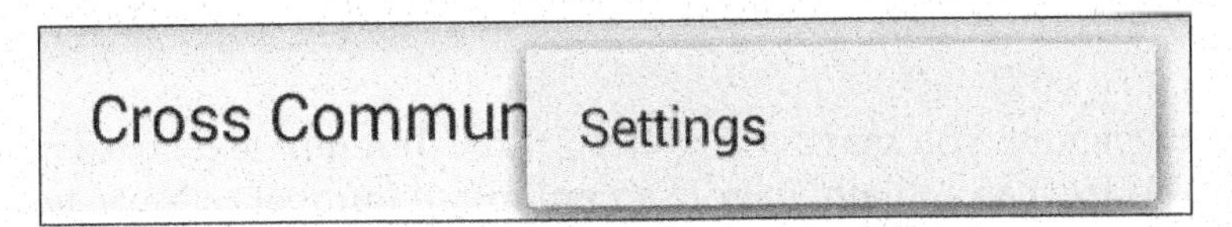

This is where we add the access to the settings screen that we just built. However, on iOS, they have no Nifty pull-down menu. So, on iOS, we will just put the settings icon (right screen). Now, I could have easily just put the settings icon on both screens, but I decided to show you how to create menus on Android in this example. Our code looks like this:

```
<ActionItem ios:icon="~/icons/ic_settings.png"
android:text="Settings" tap="settingsTap"   ios.position="right"
android.position="popup" />
```

Looking at it, you should see `ios.position`. It specifies where the `ActionItem` parameter will show up on the `ActionBar` tag on iOS devices. In Android, the position supports `popup`, which is what gives us that neat menu. In addition, you will also see that I prefixed the icon with `ios:`, which signifies that this parameter only applies on an iOS device. I did the same thing with the text property that says `settings`. We prefixed it with `android:` to make it only apply on Android devices. You can add as many `ActionItem` tags as you want to your `ActionBar` property. Then, you can complete it by adding the closing `ActionBar` tags. This completes the header part of the page, so we will continue to work on the body part of the page.

Main page body

Take a look at the preceding image again. The next item, if you guess, would be `GridLayout`. Yes, the layout you just learned to use on the settings screen. We chose a `GridLayout` here, because it can automatically make the main panel use all (remember the asterisk) the available space and make the entry panel use only the space it needs (the auto). Our code is really simple: `<GridLayout rows="*,auto" columns="*">`. We are asking for two rows and one column of data. Our next piece of the UI is another new component called `ScrollView`.

ScrollViews

Now, if you haven't guessed by its name, it allows us to scroll content either horizontally or vertically. In our case, we just need to scroll vertically so that the code looks like this: `<ScrollView id="scroller" cssClass="border">`. Now, you might have noticed that we assigned both a `cssClass` class and gave it an `id` variable. We need to be able to manipulate the `ScrollView` class later, and of course, it doesn't look as nice without the border. ScrollViews allow you to scroll as much as you want in the directions you configure, so it is great for content that won't fit inside the screen.

Looking at our picture, you may have noticed three different text boxes inside ScrollView. The app can actually handle an unlimited number of those text boxes. The next component is how we streamline, creating each one of the messages. There is a component that already does all the hard work for us. It is called the **Repeater**. Pretty original name, huh? Bet you cannot guess what it does. OL, so you did guess. It repeats a child for each item it has. So, its code looks like this: `<Repeater items="{{messages}}">`. You can either programmatically assign an array to the items or use the cool NativeScript binding system, like I did using `items="{{message}}"`. This means it will be bound to the messages variable.

More about bindings

Using an `ObservableArray` instance and binding, I made our job a whole lot simpler as when our `message` variable is bound to the `repeater` component, the `message` variable will automatically notify the `repeater` component of any changes to it. This allows our screen to stay totally in sync with the `message` array, without us having to program any additional code. Anytime we add a message, it adds it to the screen, and anytime we eliminate a message from our message queue, it is removed from the screen.

Repeaters

The next step of a repeater is to define the child template that it will use to stamp out for each item in the message array. Now, this code might look a bit complex, but you have to remember that this chunk of code displays the icon on either side, aligns the text on either side, and colorizes it to the proper color.

First, we will start out with the complex property `<Repeater.itemTemplate>`. Then, we will define the layout. Can you guess what my favorite layout is? It is `<GridLayout columns="auto,*,auto" rows="auto">`.

In our case, we are defining the grid, a single row, and three columns. The first and third columns are my columns for icons. They are set to `auto` size. If there is no icon in the column, then they would use no space. The second column, which is for the actual message, is set to use all the remaining column width.

For the first column, the code to actually display the icon might look a little strange: `<Label col="0" cssClass="{{ from === 1 || from === 2 ? 'noicon' : 'icons larger'}}" text="{{ iconleft }}"/>`. We will explain exactly how it displays a picture even though it's declared as a text label when we dig into the CSS code of this screen. I will, however, dig into the weird logic code inside the binding brackets. The binding system actually allows you some limited calculations. So, I'm using a ternary operator to check what the value of `from` parameter is. If it is `1` or `2`, then I use `noicon`; otherwise, in all other cases, I return `icons larger` as my CSS classes. Now, I could have used this logic inside the JavaScript and just used a simple variable name. However, I did it here to show you that it is possible to have dynamic changes in your Declarative UI.

Following the icon, we need to display the text message `<TextView col="1" editable="false" text="{{ message }}" cssClass="{{ from === 1 ? 'rightmessage message' : from === 2 ? 'errormessage message' : from === 0 ? 'sysmessage message' : 'leftmessage message' }}" textWrap="true"/>`. It also uses a couple of ternary operators for its CSS class definition. The class definitions are what give the messages a color.

Finally, we have the column that displays the icons on the right-hand side: `<Label col="2" cssClass="{{ from === 1 ? 'blue icons larger' : from === 2 ? 'red icons larger' : 'noicon'}}" text="{{ iconright }}"/>`. As you can see, this is just like the first icon. We just use a ternary operator to choose the proper CSS class.

Following that code, we just close the `GridLayout`, `Repeater.template`, `Repeater`, and finally, the `ScrollView` components.

Main-body footer

The next bit of code deals with the entry portion of the screen. Looking at the preceding images again, I am sure you can guess what layout I would choose? How about the number of rows and columns? If you didn't get `<GridLayout row="1" rows="*" columns="*,auto" cssClass="border">`, then repeat after me. "GridLayouts are AWESOME!" OK, back to the subject! We only need one row. We need two columns, one for the entry box and one for the cool button you can click to send our message. Taking all the bits of code scattered in this section and then putting it together looks like this:

```
<Page id="page" loaded="pageLoaded" navigatedTo="navigatedTo">
  <Page.actionBar>
    <ActionBar title="Cross Communicator">
      <ActionBar.actionItems>
        <ActionItem ios:icon="~/icons/ic_settings.png"
        android:text="Settings" tap="settingsTap"
        ios.position="right" android.position="popup" />
      </ActionBar.actionItems>
    </ActionBar>
  </Page.actionBar>
  <GridLayout rows="*,auto" columns="*">
    <ScrollView id="scroller" cssClass="border">
      <Repeater items="{{messages}}">
        <Repeater.itemTemplate>
          <GridLayout columns="auto,*,auto" rows="auto">
            <Label col="0"  cssClass="{{ from === 1 || from === 2
            ? 'noicon' : 'icons larger'}}" text="{{ iconleft }}"/>
            <TextView col="1" editable="false" text="{{ message
            }}" cssClass="{{ from === 1 ? 'rightmessage message' :
            from === 2 ? 'errormessage message' : from === 0 ?
            'sysmessage message' : 'leftmessage message' }}"
            textWrap="true"/>
            <Label col="2"  cssClass="{{ from === 1 ? 'blue icons
            larger' : from === 2 ? 'red icons larger' :
            'noicon'}}" text="{{ iconright }}"/>
          </GridLayout>
        </Repeater.itemTemplate>
      </Repeater>
    </ScrollView>
    <GridLayout row="1" rows="*" columns="*,auto"
    cssClass="border">
      <TextField id="entry" hint="Type a message"/>
      <Button id="go" col="1" text="&#xE163;" tap="goTap"
      cssClass="icons sendbutton"/>
    </GridLayout>
  </GridLayout>
</Page>
```

How about we run the screen now and see what it looks like:

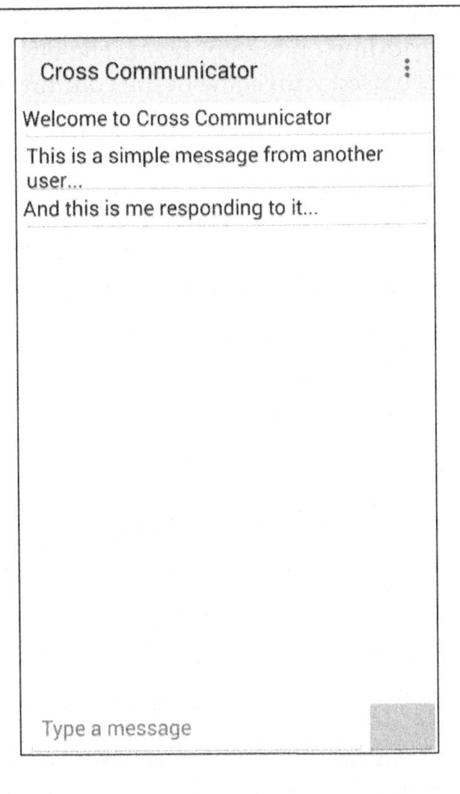

Wow, that looks a lot different from our preceding finished screen. No icons, no borders, no colorings, lines under each text, everything is left aligned, and even the bottom button is wrong. Can you guess why?

The main-page.css file

If you guess CSS, you would be correct. Let's proceed and make it look pretty. We will actually need to create a `main-page.css` file, as this file does not yet exist. The `main-page.css` file has several rules that we use to make things look pretty. We are primarily going to define padding, colors, and font sizes. So, the first thing we will do is declare rules for the `GridLayout` and `Repeater` components:

```
GridLayout, Repeater {
  padding: 2;
}
```

We just wanted is 2-pixel padding on both of them. The next thing we need to define is the `larger` rule, which we used with some of the columns to make them larger in the texts:

```
larger {
  font-size: 22;
}
```

We will now declare the default rule for all messages:

```
.message {
  padding: 5;     margin: 2;
  font-size: 12;  border-radius: 10;
}
```

You can see we just set some padding, the margin, the default font size, and finally, the border radius, which is what makes the cool curved border. Then, we will declare the colors and alignment for the four different message types:

```
.rightmessage {
  background-color: skyblue;   color: blue;  horizontal-align:
  right;
}
.errormessage {
  background-color: indianred; color: white; horizontal-align:
  right;
}
.leftmessage {
  background-color: cornsilk;  color: black; horizontal-align:
  left;
}
.sysmessage {
  background-color: cadetblue; color: white; horizontal-align:
  left;
}
```

That was pretty straightforward, and now, all the messages have awesome colors. The next chunk of CSS code deals with the width and colors of the icon columns:

```
.blue {
  color: blue;
}
.red {
  color: maroon;
}
.noicon {
  width: 90;
}
```

As you can see, we just set the color we want the icons to be, and we also set the spacing for when there is no icon, since we don't want the messages to ever hit the other side of the screen. Finally, we need to execute the CSS for the send message button at the bottom of the screen:

```
.sendbutton {
  margin: 2; width: 40; height: 40;
  border-radius: 20; background-color: gainsboro; color: black;
}
```

With this one rule, we set the button width and height to be the same size. We set the color and the border radius to make it into a circle.

We added a lot of simple CSS, setting the colors, padding, margins, and alignment. With all these small additions, we got the screen from a plain one to a nice colorful one. The last piece of this puzzle is the main application-wide CSS. We could have put the final two rules we are putting in the `app.css` file here. However, they really are better since they are global rules.

Application CSS

Start by opening your application-wide CSS, that is, the `app.css` file. We will rewrite it. First, we need to delete everything in the file. Then, we will add two items that should be globally available. The first rule we will add is a `border` rule. If you recall, we used the `border` rule in our Declarative UI to declare that the item had a border. We will define it as shown in the following code snippet:

```
.border {
  border-color: black; border-width: 1; margin: 5;
}
```

Pretty simple, anytime and anywhere we use the class border, that element will have a black border that is `1` pixel wide with a margin of `5` pixels. The next application-wide CSS we will add is the `icons` rule:

```
.icons {
  font-family: MaterialIcons-Regular, Material Icons;
  vertical-align: center;
}
```

For the icons rule, we are declaring it to be a font. We want this font to vertically align itself to the center of the column it is in. Now, this font does not exist by default on either platform. That is right! All those neat little pictures are created by this font. We are using this font since all fonts can easily scale and then you do not have to worry about different screen resolutions or sizes. If you can do it with a font instead of a graphic file, it normally makes more sense.

Fonts

Google maintains a large number of very nice fonts (`https://www.google.com/fonts`) that can be easily used for no charge in any of our applications. The one we will use for our application is the one that has all sorts of icons, some of which we will use to make our app look a lot nicer or make our app be a bit more consistent with other apps on our devices. You can download the Material Icon font from Google's GitHub repo at `https://github.com/google/material-design-icons/blob/master/iconfont/MaterialIcons-Regular.ttf`. Then, click on the RAW link, and it should download the font for you.

Once the file has finished downloading, you will need to create a new folder called `fonts` in your `app` folder, like we discussed in *Chapter 2, The Project Structure*. Then, copy the `MaterialIcons-Regular.ttf` font file into that `app/fonts` folder.

On Android and iOS, they both are currently able to auto-register the font by the name in the font-family declaration. If you look at the `font-family` declaration, it says `MaterialIcons-Regular`. The declaration value needs to be named identically as the font filename without the `.ttf` extension. The second declared font `Material Icons` is the actual internal name of the font. iOS needs to link the auto-registered font to the font you are wanting to use when you use the `icon` rule. If you double-click on the actual font file, at the top of the font, you should see `Material Icon`. So, we will declare the `icon` rule to have two font declarations: one for Android and iOS (which it uses to load it) and the second for iOS. When iOS does not see the first font in its loaded fonts, it then checks the following fonts in the list, which, of course, it will then match with the font that it loaded. This is the simplest way to use fonts on both iOS and Android. Frequently, the actual font name will match the filename. Then, you only need to put the single font declaration that will work for both platforms.

Icons

Just like Google offers a bazillion fonts, they also have a large number of icons in the `Material Icon` font, which you can see and download also as images. Since the `ActionItem` instance does not allow us to change the font, I had to use an actual graphic on iOS. In this case, I looked through the list of icons available, found a settings icon at `https://www.google.com/design/icons/#ic_settings`, then downloaded the 24dp black pngs. After opening up the ZIP file, you should see both an iOS and an Android folder. I created a new `app/icons` folder and then copied the three images out of the iOS folder and put them in the new `apps/icon` folder.

With all these changes, the app now actually looks proper. The final piece of the puzzle is the code to communicate with the server.

Communication with the server

The code we use will use to talk to the server is the nonvisual component XMLHttpRequest. This component is actually already included in the global namespace, since that is where most normal JavaScript expects it. We will create a simple class wrapper around it to communicate with the server. The first part of the class is just the initialization:

```
var AJAXSocket = function() {
  this._host = null;
  this._counter = 0;
  this._clientId = Math.floor(Math.random()*100000);
  this._from = "Unknown_"+this._clientId;
  this._messageHandler = [];
  var self = this;
  setInterval(function () {
    self._handleListener();
  }, 250);
};
exports.AJAXSocket = AJAXSocket;
```

As you can see, we set up a couple of internal variables, and then we made a `listener` function fire every 250 milliseconds to ask the server for any new updates. This is not very battery or bandwidth efficient, but with some work, it could be made a lot smarter. Then, we made sure to assign this class to the exports so that anything requiring this module will be able to use our cool class.

The next piece of code is just a couple of simple setters. We need to be able to configure the `AjaxSocket` class from outside the code:

```
AJAXSocket.prototype.setHost = function(host) {
  this._host = "http://"+host + "/direct/";
};

AJAXSocket.prototype.setName = function(name) {
  this._from = name;
};
```

The next piece is the function to send a message to the server. We will check and set up the URL we are sending our message to. Then, we will create a new `XMLHttpRequest` request, configure it, and send our message via the server:

```
AJAXSocket.prototype.send = function(msg) {
  if (!this._host) { return; }
  var url = this._host + "send/";
  if (this._clientId) {  url += "?clientId="+this._clientId;}
  var self = this;
  var request = new XMLHttpRequest();
  request.onload = function() {
    try {
      self._handler("send", request.responseText);
    } catch (e) {   }
  };
  msg.from = this._from;
  request.open("POST", url, true);
  request.send(encodeURI(JSON.stringify({from: this._from,
  message: msg})));
};
```

One thing I will point out in this function is that we treat the response we get back from a `send` request as a valid message. The server will return responses on a `check` and a `send` request.

Now that we have the ability to send messages, we need to be able to check for new messages and receive them easily. Our next code is the `listener` function that we scheduled to be every 250 ms in the class constructor:

```
AJAXSocket.prototype._handleListener = function() {
  if (!this._host) return;
  var self = this;

  var url = this._host + "get/";
  if (this._clientId) {url += "?clientId="+this._clientId;}

  var request = new XMLHttpRequest();
  request.onload = function(d) {
    self._handler("get", request.responseText);
  };
  request.onerror = function(d) {
    self._handler("error", request.status);
  };

  request.open("GET", url, true);
  request.send();
};
```

This is a fairly simple function like the sender. We verified and set up the URL. Then, we set up the two functions that will get the responses and then fire off our request to the server.

The next piece of this communication puzzle is the message-handling function, which handles all responses back from the server:

```
AJAXSocket.prototype._handler = function (event, result) {
  if (!result) return;
  var data = {};
  if (result.length > 0) {
    try {
```

```
          data = JSON.parse(result);
        }
        catch (e) { }
      }
      if (event === "get" || event === "send") {
        if (data && data.clientId && this._clientId !== data.clientId)
        {
          this._clientId = data.clientId;
        }
        for (var i=0;i<data.messages.length;i++) {
          var from = 3;
          if (data.messages[i].from === "ME") continue;
          if (data.messages[i].from === "SERVER") {
            from = 2;
          } else {
            data.messages[i].message = data.messages[i].from +": " +
            data.messages[i].message;
          }

          this.handleMessages({from: from, data:
          data.messages[i].message});
        }
      } else if (event === "abort" || event === "error") {
        this.handleMessages({from: 2, data: event});
      }
    };
```

We will check the result. If there is no result, we don't do anything. Then, we attempted to parse the result back into a JSON object. Next, we checked the type of event; a `get` or `send` event means it has some messages. We then checked to see whether the server is reassigning our `clientId` parameter; if so, we switch to it. Finally, we looked through each message that just came in and assigned it a `from` number so that our display looks correct. If the message is an `abort` or `error` message, we just spit it out to the screen as is.

The final piece of this code is the event handling, which is extremely simple:

```
AJAXSocket.prototype.handleMessages = function(msg) {
  for (var i=0;i<this._messageHandler.length;i++) {
    this._messageHandler[i](msg);
  }
};

AJAXSocket.prototype.on = function(eventName, fun) {
  this._messageHandler.push(fun);
};
```

Basically, all `handleMessages` does is loop through any listeners and send our message to them, and our `on` function just adds new listeners to the listeners array. A couple of things missing from this `AJAXSocket` class would be the getters for the `name` and `server` properties that we have setters for, and an `off` request to remove a handler. For our example, we won't use those functions, so they are not included, but feel free to extend this class to add that functionality if you need it for your project.

Trying out our application

Are you ready! Our application is now fully ready for you to actually test its functionality. It not only has a settings screen, but also has the ability to communicate with a server to exchange messages. So, the only piece missing is a server. Guess what, we have one of those too. Let's check out the next piece and get the communication server up and running.

The server

The server code itself won't be discussed in this book as it is not relevant to learning NativeScript. It is in JavaScript, so feel free to look at it. It is downloadable from the same example repo that contains all the example in this book, located at `https://github.com/GettingStartedWithNativeScript`. In the event you want to run your own server or, for some reason, the test server on `nativescript.rocks:3000` is not running, the following instructions will help you set up and connect to your own server.

Setting up your own server

To set up the server follow the given steps:

1. Once you have downloaded the ZIP file and extracted the server or used Git to clone a copy, you will just need to use a `npm install` command in its directory. This will install everything that the server needs to work. To start your server, you just need to type `node index.js`, and the server process will start up and start listening on port 3000 of your machine. As you can see from the following screenshot, I cloned the repo from GitHub, did an `npm` install and then a node index.js install. It then printed out all the IP addresses on my machine.

```
Command Prompt - node index.js

G:\Projects>git clone https://github.com/GettingStartedWithNativeScript/crossCommunicator_Server.git

Cloning into 'crossCommunicator_Server'...
remote: Counting objects: 7, done.
remote: Compressing objects: 100% (7/7), done.
remote: Total 7 (delta 0), reused 7 (delta 0), pack-reused 0
Unpacking objects: 100% (7/7), done.
Checking connectivity... done.

G:\Projects>cd crossCommunicator_Server

G:\Projects\crossCommunicator_Server>npm install
npm WARN package.json websockets-server@1.0.0 No README data
npm WARN optional dep failed, continuing utf-8-validate@1.2.1
npm WARN optional dep failed, continuing bufferutil@1.2.1
ws@0.8.0 node_modules\ws
├── options@0.0.6
└── ultron@1.0.2

G:\Projects\crossCommunicator_Server>node index.js
Wireless Network Connection 192.168.2.102
VirtualBox Host-Only Network 192.168.56.1
VMware Network Adapter VMnet1 169.254.134.128
VMware Network Adapter VMnet5 192.168.32.1
VMware Network Adapter VMnet8 192.168.92.1
VirtualBox Host-Only Network #2 192.168.155.1
Loopback Pseudo-Interface 1 127.0.0.1
Listening on port 3000
```

2. You can now open up a browser and type `localhost:3000` in your URL bar. You will see the server in a browser interface.
3. The next step is to make our `crossCommunicator` app talk to the cool server. This is where things might get a little tricky. Let's take a look at the following description:
    - On the iOS emulator, you can just use `localhost:3000` for the server. It is simple. However, if you are using an Android emulator or a physical phone, then each will have its own IP address.

  - For the Android emulator, what you will need to do is run `adb devices` (after the Android emulator is running) from the terminal to see what network address it is using. On my machine, `adb devices` comes back with **192.168.56.100:5555**. If you are using a physical Android phone, you need to go to **Settings** | **About** | **Status** and scroll down until you see the IP address.
  - On a physical iOS device, you need to go to **Settings** | **Wi-Fi** and then check the DHCP or **Static** tab for the current IP address.

4. Once you have the device or emulator IP address, you need to match it. Look at the list of IP addresses that the server process printed out that it is listening on. Whichever IP address matches the first three groups of numbers. For example, if you look at the preceding server install screenshot and then the following example `adb devices` screenshot, you will see that the second server IP address is the VirtualBox IP address **192.168.56.1**. This is the address that matches the Android emulator's IP address **192.168.56.100** that `adb devices` printed out. So that server IP address is what you want to use for the server. So, in my case, for my application settings, I would then put `192.168.56.1:3000` as the server and `Nathanael` as the name.

```
Command Prompt
G:\Projects\crossCommunicator_Server>adb devices
List of devices attached
192.168.56.100:5555     device

G:\Projects\crossCommunicator_Server>_
```

Trying crossCommunicator out.

You should be able to do a `nativescript run android -emulator` or `nativescript run ios -mulator` and then have the application start up. Once you have the server settings plugged into your app, you should be able to send and get messages from the browser and the iOS and Android platforms (basically, as many devices as you want to hook up to your server).

Summary

Wow, we covered a lot in this chapter. We explored the different types of layouts and dialogs, and learned all about promises, icons, and fonts. On top of all that cool knowledge, we built a fully running cross-platform communication system. Pretty awesome and we are only on *Chapter 4, Building a Featured Application*. Stay tuned! We will cover how to add, find, and use third-party modules in *Chapter 5, Installing Third-Party Components*, to make our application even better.

5

Installing Third-Party Components

NativeScript contains a wide range of built-in components. However, sometimes, you need things that are not built into the default NativeScript components. This is where a third-party plugin or component can come into play. A plugin can encompass any part of an application. It can be anything from simple JavaScript code that talks to the camera, to something much more complex, such as 3D charting. A plugin can be something as simple as a simple JavaScript code function or as complex as a combination of a JavaScript library and multiple compiled libraries for each specific platform.

In this chapter, we will cover the following topics:

- Places to find third-party components
- How to install a third-party component
- Using the third-party components in a cross communicator

Places to find third-party components

Currently, there are three major places to find components. Each place has its own strength and weakness. The first one that we will explore is the official Telerik plugin site.

The Telerik plugin site

You can find the Telerik plugin site at `http://plugins.telerik.com/nativescript`. This site allows different developers to list any of their available free plugins. You can search or browse the site and find many different plugins built for NativeScript.

npmjs.com

The next site is `https://npmjs.com`, and it actually contains common modules and plugins for a wide range of products, such as **Node.js**, **jQuery**, **Bower**, **Grunt**, and many more JavaScript-based products. It is the most popular JavaScript repository. On `npmjs.com`, to find plugins for NativeScript, you can just type `NativeScript` in the search box and click on the **Search** button. It will list all the items that support NativeScript. You should also see a couple of listings for the official NativeScript libraries that make up NativeScript in the list. This is because `npm` is what you used to download and install NativeScript in the first place.

The NativeScript unofficial plugin list

The third site is a simple plugin list. It lists the name, what platforms it supports, and what the plugin does. It links to the location of `npmjs.com` and/or `github.com` to download the plugin. The unique thing that this list offers is a simple list that also quickly, at a glance, lists all the platforms a plugin supports. It can be found at `http://nativescript.rocks/plugins`.

How to install a third-party plugin component

This is actually one of the more simple things to do in most cases. We will install three different plugins. The first component is just a simple plugin to vibrate the phone, which we will use for any new messages. Then, we will install a more complex plugin that we will use for real-time communication. Finally, we will install a visual component. By choosing these three examples, I hope to show you a small subset of the available features that you can easily install to gain new functionality for your application.

Installing the vibration plugin

By exploring any of those three plugin sites, you should find a plugin called `nativescript-vibrate`. This is the plugin we will use to handle the vibration. To install a plugin, you need to be connected to the Internet. Then, all we need to do is simply type `nativescript plugin add nativescript-vibrate` in the root project directory. This will automatically download and install all the code for the vibration plugin into the main project `node_modules` folder. This is a pure JavaScript plugin, so if you navigate to the `node_modules` | `nativescript-vibrate` folder, you can easily see how it works.

You don't normally want to edit a plugin's source code directly in this folder, because when you reinstall the plugin, you will lose all your changes. If you actually need to make a change to a plugin, it is much better to fork the original repo and then install the plugin from your own forked repo.

A forked repo means you make a copy of the source code that matches the source code as it exists in that moment of time. When the original author continues editing the source, their code will go in one direction, and if you edit your copy of the source, your copy goes in the other direction. This concept is just like a fork in the road. The nice thing about source control is that you can typically easily merge forks.

Installing the webSockets plugin

Again, if you search any of the three plugin sites, you should find a plugin called `nativescript-websockets`. To install this plugin, you simply type `nativescript plugin add nativescript-websockets` in the root project directory. This will also automatically download the plugin and install all the files where they need to be located. This plugin also includes a compiled library for both Android and iOS, which gets built into your application automatically.

Installing the Telerik SideDrawer plugin

The installation of this plugin is identical to the other two. We can search for NativeScript-Telerik-UI and then install it via `nativescript plugin add nativescript-telerik-ui` in the root project directory. As usual, you must be connected to the Internet for the first time so that it can be downloaded and installed.

Using third-party components

Once we have all the plugins installed, the next step is to actually use each of the plugins. We will need to open your `main-page.js` file and add some code to use the plugin inside your application's main page.

Using the vibration plugin

We will start with this cool feature first. We want to make the device vibrate when a new message comes in. First, we just need to add the code to load the vibration component. Open the `main-page.js` file. At the top of the file near the other required statements, you need to add a simple new require statement, `var vibrate = require('nativescript-vibrate');`. Since all the messages already go through a central `newMessage` function, let's add this code at the very bottom of this function:

```
if (msg.from !== 1) {
  vibrate.vibration(100);
}
```

This code simply checks to see that the message doesn't come from us. After all, we don't really want to make the phone vibrate on our own messages. It then uses the `vibrate` class that we required a couple of sentences ago and runs the vibration command. The device takes 100 milliseconds to vibrate. Just by adding and using a plugin, we quickly added a nifty notification feature. Pretty cool, huh? Let's now start tackling the bigger plugin. We will replace our simple Ajax-based communication with real-time websockets.

Using Websockets

Our Ajax class was a cool place to start, and it gave you a concrete example of how to use the HTTP class. However, it is not battery or server friendly, and it has to keep creating and opening a new connection to the server and then asking the server, "Hey, do you have any messages for me?" Websockets was designed to allow you to open a connection to the server once, which just stays open. Then, either side can use this connection to send messages to the other side. This is not only vastly more reliable, but also battery and server friendly and, best of all, totally real time.

To switch and use real-time websockets, we will create a small wrapper around websockets to make it so that we can use either Ajax requests or websockets. This way, you can easily play with either to do any additional experimenting easily.

So, replace `var Socket = require('AjaxSocket')` with `var Socket = require('WebSocketWrapper')`. This will load our new wrapper for websockets after we create it. If you want to play with the Ajax socket again, you just need to switch this one line of code back. The `WebSocketWrapper` code will be similar to the `AjaxSocket` library. We want to maintain the same function interface so that we can use either just by acquiring it.

First of all, we need to create a new file called `WebSocketWrapper.js`, and then, we need to add the code to load the `websocket` plugin. So, the first line of code would be `var WS = require('nativescript-websockets');`, as it loads the websockets component that we installed earlier in the chapter. Then, we need to create our class, which should look like this:

```
var WebSocketWrapper = function() {
  this._host = null;
  this._backoff = 100;
  this._timeoutId = null;
  this._clientId = null;
  this._from = "Unknown_"+Math.floor(Math.random()*100000);
  this._messageHandler = [];
  this._websocket = null;
  this._errorCount = 0;
};
```

As you can see, this looks similar to our Ajax socket class. The differences really have to do with us adding a back-off ability to the reconnect code for websockets in the case of errors. Back-off means that if it fails to connect (or gets disconnected), rather than retrying immediately all the time, it slowly lengthens the delay between each of the connection attempts. If it was a single glitch, you would then be connected immediately. However, when you enter a dead zone, it will lengthen each additional attempt to connect so that your battery life is saved.

Next, we need to add the same setters, `setHost` and `setName`:

```
WebSocketWrapper.prototype.setHost = function(host) {
  this._host = "ws://"+host;
  if (this._websocket && this._websocket.isOpen()) {
    this._websocket.close();
  }
  this._openSocket();
};
WebSocketWrapper.prototype.setName = function(name) {
  this._from = name;
};
```

As you can see, `setName` is exactly the same as we had in the Ajax library, and `setHost` only has a couple minor changes. The first change is to use `ws://` instead of `http://` as `ws` denotes websockets. The second change is to close the existing websocket, if it is open. Finally, we need to actually open a new websocket connection when the host is changed. The next piece of code we need to add is the `send` function:

```
WebSocketWrapper.prototype.send = function(msg) {
  if (!this._websocket) { return; }
  var message = {from: this._from, message: msg};
  if (this._clientId) {
    message.clientId = this._clientId;
  }
  this._websocket.send(JSON.stringify(message));
};
```

Wow, this code is a lot smaller than the Ajax version. The reason is because our websocket is already open, and all we have to do is send the message to the server in the format the server expects. In our case, the message is a simple JSON structure. The last function that we have to add to match the same function interface is the `on` function:

```
WebSocketWrapper.prototype.on = function(eventName, fun) {
  this._messageHandler.push(fun);
};
```

This code is identical to what we used in the Ajax socket wrapper. All we are doing is pushing our `event` function into the event queue the same way. With these four functions, we now have a library that contains the exact same function interface as the Ajax socket library. This means it is functionally compatible. However, we still have to create some of the internal functions such as `_openSocket`, which we referenced from the `setHost` function. So, let's look at these created functions next:

```
WebSocketWrapper.prototype._openSocket = function() {
  var self = this;
  // This function does back-off re-connection
  var retryConnection = function() {
    // If we already have one scheduled; then we don't need
    // to do anything more.
    if (self._timeoutId) return;
```

```
    // The actual function that opens up the websocket
    // that gets scheduled in the future
    self._timeoutId = setTimeout(function() {
      self._timeoutId = null;
      self._websocket.open(); // Open Websocket
    }, self._backoff);

    // Take our current back off time, and add random amount
    // up to 1 second of time
    self._backoff += Math.floor(Math.random()*1000);

    // set the max back off time to be 10,000 milliseconds.
    if (self._backoff > 10000) {
      self._backoff = 10000;
    }
  };

  // Create a new websocket
  this._websocket = new WS(this._host);

  // Create a handler for any new messages that come in.
  this._websocket.on('message', function(socket, msg) {
    self._handler(msg);
  });

  // This gets called when the websocket is successfully opened
  // We use it to reset the back-off and error counts.
  this._websocket.on('open', function() {
    self._errorCount = 0;
    self._backoff = 100;
  });

  // On any errors, we only want to print the first error.
  this._websocket.on('error', function(socket, msg) {
    self._errorCount++;
    if (self._errorCount === 1) {
      self._handleMessages({from: 2, data: msg});
    }
  });
```

```
    // If the socket is closed, and it isn't a normal close
    // then we need to run reopen the connection
    this._websocket.on('close', function(socket, code) {
      if (self._websocket === socket && code !== 1000) {
        retryConnection();
      }
    });

    // Open our web socket.
    this._websocket.open();
  };
```

Now, this function is fairly large, but the majority of the code actually is used for our cool back-off ability to recover a broken connection without wasting a lot of battery. It also has a little extra code to report any errors in the connection. In the preceding code, we also added an inner function called `retryConnection`, which automatically schedules a function sometime randomly in the future so that each time it fails, it takes a bit longer to try again. Technically, if we wanted to make this function simpler, the only code that is actually needed to make everything work in the `_openSocket` function is as follows:

```
    this._websocket = new WS(this._host);
    this._websocket.on('message', function(socket, msg) {
      self._handler(msg);
    });
    this._websocket.open();
```

As all we actually need is to create a new websocket, set up the message handler and then finally open the connection. For better battery life and additional reliability, having the extra code that allows back-off to reconnect is used. The next function we need to create is our message handler, which is aptly called the `_handler` function. It looks like this:

```
  WebSocketWrapper.prototype._handler = function (result) {
    // If we have no result; then just exit.
    if (!result || !result.length) return;

    // Attempt to parse the JSON packet
    var data = {};
    try {
      data = JSON.parse(result);
    }
    catch (e) { }
```

```
    // Commands from Server
    if (data && data.command) {
      switch (data.command) {
        case "setClient": this._clientId = data.clientId;
      break;

      }
      return;
    }

    // Any messages from me, we just ignore since we already
    // Handle it internally before sending it to the server.
    if (data.from === "ME") return;

    // Figure out who the message is from.
    var from = 3;
    if (data.from === "SERVER") {
      from = 2;
    } else {
      data.message = data.from +": " + data.message;
    }

    // Now that we have our message all setup, trigger the event
    this._handleMessages({from: from, data: data.message});

  };
```

This function is a bit more complex than our Ajax version. The reason for this is that it was designed to allow us to extend the protocol easily to allow you to send images, sound, and pretty much anything else you want. It also has a command channel that allows the server to send information for the program to handle without any user involvement. In this case, `clientId` is actually set from the server rather than generated randomly in the Ajax version. You can now easily enhance this program and server to allow pretty much anything you want to transfer. We are almost done with this. The `_handler` function calls `_handleMessages`, so we need to create this function next:

```
WebSocketWrapper.prototype._handleMessages = function(msg) {
  for (var i=0;i<this._messageHandler.length;i++) {
    this._messageHandler[i](msg);
  }
};
```

This code is also identical to the Ajax socket library. It goes through every registered event listener and calls it with the new message. The final step in our wrapper is to export it, so the final line of code will be `module.exports = WebSocketWrapper;`. This line of code allows us to use the created class when we execute the `require('WebSocketWrapper');` method. It was pretty simple to wrap the websockets for use in our application. Let's proceed to add the final plugin to our application.

Using Telerik's side drawer

Now, a visual plugin is used differently than a non-visual plugin. In the preceding two cases, we used `require` to load the component and then used that component. To use a visual plugin, we open the Declarative UI file in which we will use it. We need to open the `main-page.xml` file and make some changes to it. First, on the very first line, that is, the `Page` declaration line, we will add `xmlns:tsd="nativescript-telerik-ui/sidedrawer"` to the declaration. This addition tells NativeScript that the `tsd` namespace is the side drawer JavaScript.

> The `tsd` namespace is just a short name for Telerik Side Drawer. We can name this namespace according to our wish. This name is used so that the XML parser knows that `RadSideDrawer` is actually associated with the code in the `nativescript-telerik-ui | sidedrawer` file.

When NativeScript loads this Declarative UI file, it will see that declaration and automatically load the `sidedrawer.js` file. The next thing we will do is add the `</Page.ActionBar>` statement right after the closing, and before the `<GridLayout ...>` statement, we will add the following declarations:

```
<tsd:RadSideDrawer title="crossCommunicator" id="sidebar">
  <tsd:RadSideDrawer.drawerContent>
   <StackLayout backgroundColor="#FFFFFF">
     <Label text="Welcome to crossCommunicator" />
      <StackLayout height="1" backgroundColor="#c7c875"/>
      <Label text="The websockets library on Android is Copyright
      (c) 2010-2012 Nathan Rajlich"/>
      <Label text="The websockets library on iOS is Copyright (c)
      2014 Zwopple Limited"/>
      <Label text="The NativeScript websockets library is
      Copyright (c) 2015 Master Technology" textWrap="true"/>
    </StackLayout>
  </tsd:RadSideDrawer.drawerContent>
<tsd:RadSideDrawer.mainContent>
```

Then, at the end of the file, right before the </Page>, we will add the following lines of code:

```
</tsd:SideDrawer.mainContent>
</tsd:SideDrawer>
```

The `RadSideDrawer` class actually wraps our content, so that is why we added the declarations around our existing content. However, the key piece is `<tsd:RadSideDrawer>`. It causes the Declarative UI to instantiate `RadSideDrawer` from the `tsd` namespace file. If the `node_modules | sidedrawer.js` file had more components than just the side drawer in it, then you could also execute a `<tsd:someOtherComponent>` method. This would create the `someOtherComponent`. These components can be created just like any other native components. They are all treated exactly the same way, other than the namespace prefix, so that the Declarative UI knows where to get the component from.

The Telerik side drawer has two parts: the actual drawer that is hidden until shown and then the main content part. We put everything we want in the side drawer inside the `drawerContent` declaration and then put all the normal main content in the `mainContent` declaration. The nice thing about the Telerik side drawer is that you can create complex layouts in the drawer just as you can in the main content area. The next time you run your application, you can now pull from the left-hand side of the screen, and you will see a simple side menu that looks like this:

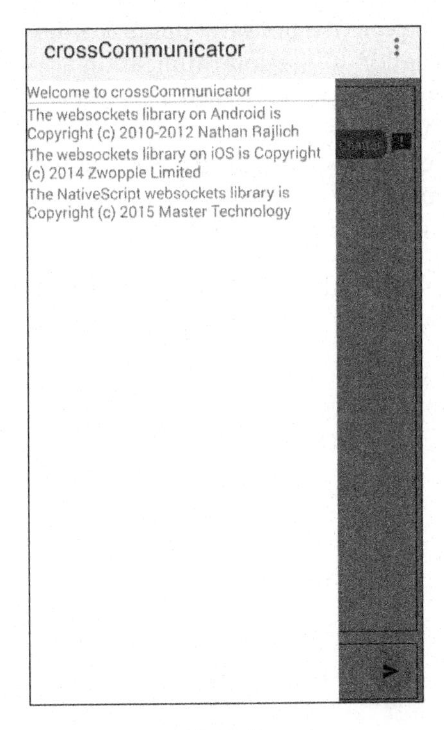

Easily using the components

As you can see, it is easy to use both visual and code-only components. They all are installed exactly the same way using the nativescript plugin add <plugin name> command. Depending on the type of component, you use the command using var myName=require(<plugin name>); and/or by telling the Declarative UI about the location of the xmlns:myname="node_modules/myname" component. After that, the code is used identically, as if you had written the code yourself.

Useful third-party components

Now that you have seen how easy it is to add plugins, you might also try adding sound effects using the cool nativescript-sound plugin or adding a database to save all your chats using nativescript-sqlite. Perhaps, add Google Maps so that you can send coordinates and have them show up on a map using the nativescript-google-sdk plugin. There are several plugins, meaning that you can add several features and experiment with them on your own communication platform. If you get rich making the next generation chat platform, you are more than welcome, at any point in time, to send me any money you want to donate!

Summary

We covered a lot in this chapter. We not only made the device vibrate but also added real-time communication to the communication app. We set up the code so that we can play and extend the application easily. You also learned how to install any of the third-party components. Depending on your application, at a minimum, you will probably use at least one of the third-party components or the side drawer in your own awesome application. As you can see, there are a lot of third-party functionalities that you can add to your app with minimal work.

Hang on! We will next look at all the different device dependencies. In the next chapter, you will understand how to make your application as device independent as possible.

6
Platform Differences

Since NativeScript wraps components on each of the platforms in a consistent fashion, there are some differences between each implementation. The actual underlying native components are implemented differently by Apple and Google engineers. You will understand how to deal with the differences in platforms and with the differences in devices on each platform.

In this chapter, we will cover the following topics:

- Android and iOS differences
- Code differences
- Platform class
- Declarative UI
- Platform- and device-specific files
- Screen size differences
- Device differences

Android and iOS differences

Since each of the platforms is implemented by totally different teams, each platform has its own particular awesome and horrible behavior. When possible, NativeScript wraps them all up and attempts to make a cohesive whole that works in a similar way on both platforms. This means for the most part, the component will work identically, but there can be discrepancies, which you may have to take into consideration. We will look at a couple of differences in depth.

The soft keyboard

One difference that you might have already noticed in our `crossCommunicator` application is that on Android, when you click on the text entry box and the soft keyboard pops up, the message log part of the screen automatically shrinks and the text entry box is still visible. This is something that Google engineers built into Android. We get this awesome behavior for free. However, on iOS, when the soft keyboard appears, it just goes over everything on the bottom part of the screen. In this case, we get this horrible behavior for free on iOS. Fortunately, it is easy to work around this issue. We can install a cool plugin called `NativeScript-IQKeyboardManager`. We can easily install this plugin the same way as the other plugins we installed. The documentation for this awesome plugin is at `https://www.npmjs.com/package/nativescript-iqkeyboardmanager`. It wraps up a technique to move the text entry field into view on iOS devices. This will allow us to have our app work in the desired way on both platforms.

The Page.loaded event

Another thing that struck me is that in *Chapter 5, Installing Third-Party Components*, we created a `showDialog` function, but you will notice that we called it from the `Page.navigatedTo` event. When I first created the application, I had it open from the `Page.loaded` event, as the loaded event makes a lot more sense to me for opening the settings dialog. The application ran perfectly on Android, and life was good. I copied it to the iOS, and it crashed immediately. Life was not so good anymore.

After spending a bit of time examining the error call stack, I figured out in the `Page.loaded` event on iOS that when an event is fired, the frame information is not fully built. The `page.showModal()` call inside our `showDialog` function requires access to the frame. When you try to do anything that requires access to the frame, it will fail. In this specific case, it totally crashed the application. The solution was to move the settings dialog code to the final page event. This way, the frame information was fully built.

This also affects executing code such as `frame.topmost().getViewById('someId')` from the `Page.loaded` event since the frame is not fully set up on iOS. If you need to find a component by ID, use `args.object` that is passed into the `Page.loaded` event as it actually points to the built page. The `frame.topmost().getViewById` method will return null in the `Page.Loaded` event.

It is very important to test the functionality on all platforms, as sometimes, it will work perfectly on your primary development platform but fail spectacularly on the other platforms.

Code differences

In cases where you are coding an Android- or iOS-specific feature or, perhaps, working around an issue on a specific platform, there is an easy technique to determine the platform on every component. Each component that wraps a native component has either an `.ios` or an `.android` property that is used to access the actual underlying native component. If we wanted to select all the text inside the `myText` text box, we can do so as follows:

```
var myText = frame.topmost().getViewById('myText');
if (myText.android) {
  console.log('We are running on Android');
  myText.android.selectAll();
} else if (myText.ios) {
  console.log("We are running on iOS");
  var range = new NSRange();
  range.location = 0;
  range.length = myText.text.length;
  myText.ios.selectedRange = range;
}
```

If you want only the code to be executed on iOS, check for the `.ios` property on the component and then add whatever the specific code is for iOS. On Android, it is the `.android` property. Each platform has its own unique property. This technique is good for the `app.js` file. Frequently, you might have to initialize a bit of code only on iOS or Android. You can use `application.ios` or `application.android` in the `app.js` file to detect the platform, as we did to initialize the material icons font on iOS in *Chapter 4, Building a Featured Application*.

Another use for the `.ios` and `.android` properties is when you need to customize a component for a specific platform. An easy example is early on in NativeScript, the background color of the iOS application was not working properly. So, to fix this, I added this code to my main page:

```
var iosFrame = frame.topmost().ios;
if (iosFrame) {
  iosFrame.controller.view.window.backgroundColor =
  UIColor.blackColor();
}
```

All it does is get the native iOS `Frame` element. If this is successful, then we are on a iOS platform. We will then use the `ObjectiveC` property to navigate to the window's background color, and we will set it to black.

Platform classes

For much more detailed platform- or device-specific information, a platform class is provided with NativeScript and is used like this:

```
var platform = require("platform");
// Device Specifics
console.log("Manufacturer:", platform.device.manufacturer);
console.log("Platform os:", platform.device.os);
console.log("Os version:", platform.device.osVersion);
console.log("Model:", platform.device.model);
console.log("SDK Version:", platform.device.sdkVersion);
console.log("Device Type:", platform.device.deviceType);
console.log("uuid:", platform.device.uuid);
console.log("Language:", platform.device.language);

// Screen Specifics
console.log("Screen width in pixels:",
platform.screen.mainScreen.widthPixels);
console.log("Screen height in pixels:", platform.screen.mainScreen.
heightPixels);
console.log("Screen width in DIPs:",
platform.screen.mainScreen.widthDIPs);
console.log("Screen height in DIPs:",
platform.screen.mainScreen.heightDIPs);
console.log("Screen scale:", platform.screen.mainScreen.scale);
```

After running the preceding code, you will output what is summarized in the following table:

iPhone Simulator	Android Simulator
Manufacturer: Apple Platform os: iOS Os version: 8.2 Model: iPhone Simulator SDK version: 8.2 Device type: Phone uuid: 40C4A1CE-88E0-4F36-85A4-9DDA7DF6B436 Language: en Screen width in pixels: 640 Screen height in pixels: 960 Screen width in DIPs: 320 Screen height in DIPs: 480 Screen scale: 2	Manufacturer: Genymotion Platform os: Android Os version: 4.4.4 Model: Samsung Galaxy S5 - 4.4.4 - API 19 - 1080x1920 SDK version: 19 Device type: Phone uuid: 5634589f2589e5f2 Language: en_US Screen width in pixels: 1080 Screen height in pixels: 1920 Screen width in DIPs: 360 Screen height in DIPs: 640 Screen scale: 3

As you can see, you can get quite a bit of information from the device you are running on. If you are checking the languages, notice that iOS returns **en** whereas Android returns **en_US**. Make sure you consider this when comparing and setting your application language from the `platform.device.language` value.

Declarative UI

You have several ways to deal with platform specifics in your Declarative UI files. We will look at each way and examine the pros and cons of each method.

Declarative UI properties

The first way is for properties. You can use the following line of code:

```
<Button ios:text="iOS is Awesome" android:text="Android is
Awesome"/>
```

As you can see, we prefixed the text property with a `ios:` or `android:` prefix, so on their respective platforms, they will declare that the platform is `Awesome`. If you only have a couple of properties to change, this is the easiest method to use and maintain. It does not allow you to change any platform-specific components though. If you have a lot of platform-specific properties or you need to use a different component on the platforms, then you will need to use Declarative UI platform qualifiers.

Declarative UI platform qualifiers

A Declarative UI platform qualifier allows you to qualify a whole group of components or properties to a specific platform like this:

```
<Page><StackLayout>
<ios><Label text="I am only on iOS"/></ios>
<android><Label text="I am only on Android"/></android>
</StackLayout></Page>
```

If you notice, we wrapped our `<Label>` components in the `<ios>` and `<android>` components. The `<ios>` and `<android>` components are not real components. "What?", you might wonder. Yeah, I know they look like how we add a component, but they are actually special Declarative UI nodes to allow you to wrap any parts of the UI that needs to be a distinct per platform. All nodes and properties between the start `<ios>` node and end `</ios>` node will only be processed and used on an iOS platform. The same applies for the `<android>` opening and closing tags. Wow! This can really allow some cool customizations in files. You can easily have different components make up a screen for each platform. Note that you cannot wrap `<ios>` inside `<android>` or `<android>` in `<ios>`. First, it does not make any sense, but second, they are mutually exclusive. There are no Apple Android or Google iOS devices. As you can see, using qualifiers is a good way to handle cases where you have a different component here or there. If you have a lot of changes between the platforms, using platform-specific files is your best bet.

Platform- and device-specific files

The last method to differentiate between platforms is through platform- and device-specific files. These qualifiers are applicable to JavaScript, CSS, and the Declarative UI XML files. You can prefix the extension of a file with `.android` or `.ios`, so the file is `main-file.ios.js` or `main-file.android.xml`. Then, only this version of the file will be loaded on that specific platform. Once the version is loaded it allows you to have a completely custom JavaScript, CSS, or Declarative UI for each platform.

In addition to the platform qualifiers, you can also use device qualifiers such as `.land` for landscape or `.port` for portrait. For screen sizes, the qualifiers `minH`, `min`, and `minWH` appended with a minimum number of pixels are used as qualifiers. So, the `main-page.minH300.css` would require the device to have at least 300 pixels height for this CSS file to load. The `.minHW400` qualifier would require that both the width and height be greater or equal to 400 pixels for that specific file to load. Be aware that when you switch orientations, NativeScript does NOT load any other version of the file. Therefore, when NativeScript loaded the landscape version of the file and then you rotate your device, the landscape version of that file is still the file that is running even though you are now in portrait mode. By mixing and using the different qualifiers, it makes it easy to customize all your screens per platform, screen size, or orientation with NativeScript.

Screen size differences

Now, in most cases, the completely different screen sizes can be handled using the platform screen size `.minW` or `minH` qualifiers so that you can build a custom layout when you are dealing with tablets versus a phone-sized device. Unfortunately, this is not always the case for any image you might want to show. In this case, you have to do a bit of manual work. Each image has a set resolution. The larger the resolution of the image, the more memory it takes, but on higher resolution devices, images obviously look much better. You can deal with images in one of the following three ways to try and make your application look the best on all devices.

Fonts

The first is the way we did in `crossCommunicator`. We used an icon font that has all the images we needed as a font character. Fonts are scalable, so irrespective of the resolution of the screen, the font renders and looks really nice. To make an even smaller font file, there are several websites, such as `http://icomoon.io`, where you can create your own custom font by combining different icons or characters from multiple fonts into a single font name. By reducing the number of glyphs (or characters) in a font, the font file size can be reduced drastically. If it is a single color image that you need, fonts are typically the best way to do it.

Our own custom resource folders

We created our own custom resource folders in our `crossCommunicator` application. We used this way for the settings icon on iOS. We created our own folder for all our icon resources and stored the icons we needed in that folder. You can do this with any resource you want, but in our case, we needed images.

If you pulled my version of the `crossCommunicator` application from the GitHub repo at `https://github.com/GettingStartedWithNativeScript`, you would see I have not only an `ic_settings.png` image file, but a `ic_setting@2x.png` image file and a `ic_settings@3x.png` image file. Apple designed iOS to automatically pull the best image for the device you are viewing it on. On the current retina (high-resolution) iOS device, the `ic_settings@2x.png` file will be automatically loaded even though we only requested the `ic_settings.png` file. The `@2x` prefix stands for double resolution. So, if your `ic_settings` file is 48 x 48, then the `ic_settings@2x.png` file should be 96 x 96 and `@3x` would be 144 x 144.

If you look at the following image, you can see what happens if you don't provide a prescaled image when an image is scaled up. The first or left image is scaled up from the normal `ic_settings.png` file size. The second or middle image is scaled up from the `ic_settings@2x.png` file. The third or right image is in its own native resolution. Which icon do you think looks the best? Which icon makes your app look sharp?

All you really need is the normal file and the `@2x.png` file. However, my opinion is that with the way computers and phones quickly change, it won't be long until Apple starts using `@3x` for an even higher resolution display. So, in this case, I am attempting to future proof this icon on `crossCommunicator` since the added size for the additional icon to the app is incredibly minuscule. Now, if you are doing much larger images, then you probably should skip `@3x` as it just bloats the app for no good reason at this point.

> I wrote this section of text before Apple released the iPhone 6s. Guess what Apple did with the 6s? They now use those mystical `@3x` icons. I decided to leave this text as is to show you that sometimes, you want to attempt to future proof your application, as it can sometimes be a wise decision. The current Apple icon guidelines are at `https://developer.apple.com/library/prerelease/ios/documentation/UserExperience/Conceptual/MobileHIG/IconMatrix.html`.

Using our own custom `resource` folder, the files in it are cross platform. I can also load the same `ic_setting.png` file on an Android device using the same path. However, Android doesn't know about `@2x`, so it would always load the normal small resolution file, which, like the preceding image, will look bad on a higher resolution display. This brings us to the third and the best way to acquire image resources.

Compiled application resources on iOS

Each platform has its own way to embed resources in the application. The way NativeScript attempts to help you is it has a folder called `App_Resources`. In the `App_Resources` folder is a subfolder for each platform. On iOS, this folder basically contains the application icons at different resolutions (including the `@2x` versions) and the default loading screen (also including the `@2x` versions). Right now, you can replace the default loading image and icons to create your own on iOS, just by replacing those image files in the `ios` folder with your own.

Now, to add additional resources, you will need to copy your additional resources into this folder. Then, you need to run the `nativescript prepare ios` command in a shell window. This will copy any new resources to the proper build folder in the platform folder. Each time you compile or prepare your application, these resources will automatically be updated from this folder to the proper build folders. Next, you will need to open up the main Xcode project (remember, it is in the `/platforms/ios` folder) and then open up the application project on the left pane. Then, open the `resources` folder as the following screenshot shows:

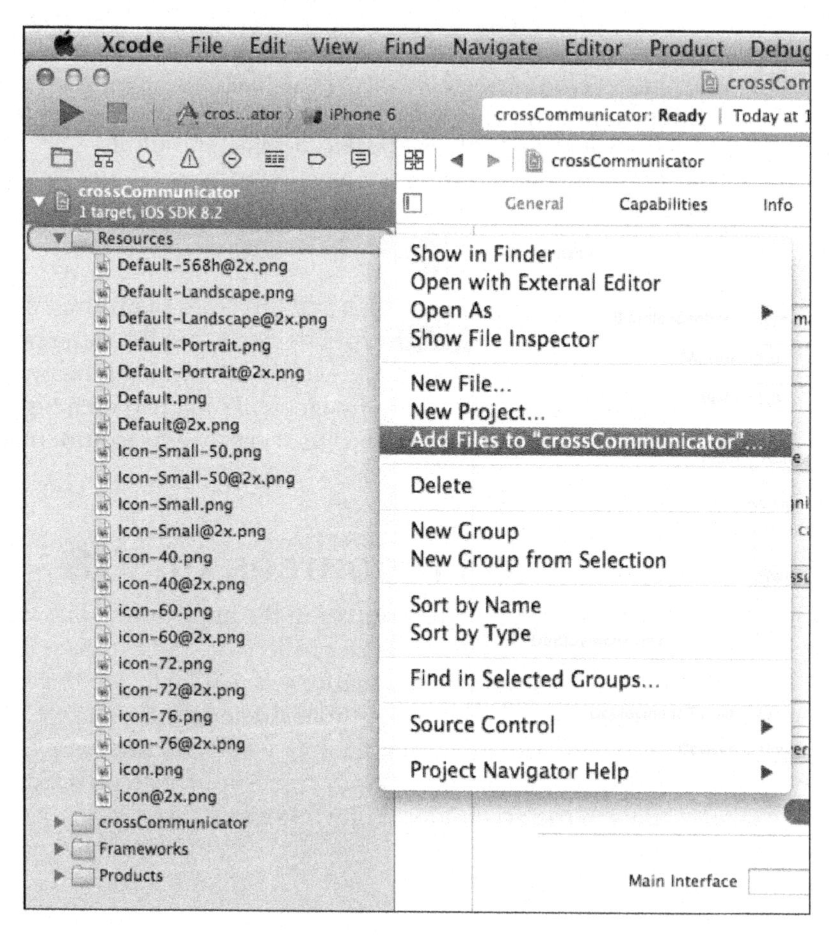

As you can see, each of the resources in your /App_Resources/ios folder are listed in this list. Then, you need to *Ctrl* + right-click the mouse to bring up the context menu on the resources folder. Then, click on the **Add Files to "crossCommunicator"...** menu option. After that, you need to navigate to the /platforms/ios/crossCommunicator/Resources folder, as this is where NativeScript puts any of your iOS resources for building. Finally, choose the resources you want to embed in your application. To show you how this works, add the ic_settings.png and ic_settings@2x.png files to the compiled resources. Then, go ahead and quit out of Xcode. After that, open up the main_page.xml file and let's change the icon to load from a resource. Line 5 should say <ActionItem ios:icon="~/icons/ ic_settings.png" ...>. Change ios:icon to <ActionItem ios:icon="res:// ic_settings.png" ...>. The res:// sufix tells NativeScript to load this from the compiled resources. That is pretty simple. The main thing you have to remember is to tell the Xcode project about your new resources. Now, let's take a look at the Android side of resources.

Compiled application resources on Android

The other folder in the App_Resources folder is android. However, once you navigate into this folder, you will see multiple drawable-??dpi folders. Each of these folders is for a different pixel density. Android breaks things down into multiple resolutions, with each lower resolution working as a fallback to the higher resolution. For example, the ldpi folder uses a 36 x 36 image for its application icon, where hdpi uses a 72 x 72 image for its application icon. Android OS automatically uses the closest folder to its resolution and then proceeds to use the next resolution until it finds the highest resolution file of the name you wanted to load.

So, if I was going to use the same ic_settings.png file on Android, I would have a 24 x 24 image (same as the normal ic_settings.png file on iOS) in the mdpi folder. Then, in the hdpi folder, it would be 36 x 36, and xhdpi would be 48 x 48 (the same as the @2x file). In xxhdpi, it would be 72 x 72, and finally, in xxxhdpi, it would be 96 x 96. So the resolutions in order are ldpi, mdpi, tvdpi, hdpi, xhdpi, xxhdpi, xxxhdpi. Any image you use, you typically want to have multiple sizes for the different Android screen resolutions. Now, you can get away with not having each of those sizes, as the Android OS will automatically scale down and scale up images from the next closest sizes. However, with icons, it might be worth having a specific icon for each size if the file size is tiny just to make your interface as sharp as possible on all devices.

On Android, those folders are as shown in this table:

	ldpi	mdpi	tvdpi	hdpi	xhdpi	xxhdpi	xxxhdpi
Scaling	0.75	1	1.33	1.5	2	3	4
Pixel Density	120	160	213	240	320	480	640
Launcher Icon Size	36 x 36	48 x 48	64 x 64	72 x 72	96 x 96	144 x 144	192 x 192

By default, `mdpi` is the default 1 pixel = 1 device independent pixel. So, when you are creating an image that you want to have in a higher resolution, multiply your dimensions by the scaling factor, and you will see what resolution you need for the other DPI sizes. For example, if we take an `mdpi` launcher icon, which is 48 x 48 and multiply 48 by the `xhdpi` scaling factor of 2, you get 96 x 96. Another example would be if you had a 100 x 120 image you were showing on `mdpi` and you wanted to be able to support `xxhdpi`, then you would take *100 * 3 = 300* and *120 * 3 = 360*. This means you want an image of 300 x 360 for `xxhdpi`.

The `mdpi` image is also equivalent to your default image size on iOS. The `xhdpi` is equivalent to the `@2x` on iOS. To my knowledge at the time of the writing this book, there is no device that takes advantage of `xxxhdpi`, just like no iOS device takes advantage of `@3x`. In addition, unless you are specifically targeting a TV device, you can ignore `tvdpi` and just use `hdpi`. The images from `hdpi` will automatically be scaled down on devices that need `tvdpi`, and the scaling down should not produce any noticeable artifacts like scaling up does.

The other nice thing you can do in the `App_Resources` folder for Android is use any of the other standard resource files and folders, such as `anim`, `color`, `layout`, `raw`, `values`, and `xml`. Each of these resource folders is treated the same way as in a traditional Java-based Android application.

On the Android platform, you do not have to do anything besides putting the resources into the folders, and you are good to go. All the resources will automatically be built into the application for you. You access the resources the same way on Android as on iOS using the `res://` prefix and then your filename. This allows you to put the same resources into both platforms and then access them exactly the same way.

In a nutshell, on iOS, make sure you have the normal and `@2x` versions of all images. On Android, you can use the normal version in the `mdpi` folder and the `@2x` version in the `xhdpi` folder (just make sure to remove `@2x` from the filename on Android). Then, your images should look fairly clean on almost all devices.

Device differences

Now that you have got a handle on how to build the resources into your application, the final item is dealing with physical differences in devices. You never know what type of device your application will be running on. The only thing you can really count on in a device is that the device will have a screen. The best impression you can give your customers is an app that doesn't crash, even if it doesn't support the device they are trying to run it on.

Each device will have different sensors and different accessories, and some might even have a physical keyboard. Take the Samsung Galaxy S4 phone. It came with sensors to detect altitude, humidity, and temperature. You might guess that the Samsung Galaxy S5 would also have the same sensors. When Samsung released their new flagship phone, they actually removed or disabled the Humidity and Temperature sensors. Fast forward to the new Samsung Galaxy S6, they now removed SD card support. Despite being flagship devices, Samsung has added and removed things through the iterations of each phone. So, before you call your code to open a connection to the GPS system, check to see whether the device actually has a GPS. On Android, the method is simple, as shown here:

```
var application = require('application');
var packageManager =
application.android.context.getPackageManager();
var hasGPS =
packageManager.hasSystemFeature(android.content.pm.PackageManager.
FEATURE_LOCATION_GPS);
```

`FEATURE_LOCATION_GPS` is one of many strings you can pass in to find out whether a specific sensor exists. If you look in the `PackageManager` documentation (`http://developer.android.com/reference/android/content/pm/PackageManager.html`), it lists all the different sensors and features you can detect on Android. On iOS, you have a much smaller number of devices. You can actually easily use the device ID from the platform module to determine whether the device supports a feature. Alternatively, when you attempt to initialize the device, make sure you have it in `try` and `catch` statements and evaluate the failures, as iOS typically throws an error stating that device ability doesn't exist.

The more often you make these verification checks and wrap the initialization in `try` and `catch` statements, the more likely your app will not crash when that support is missing. So, verify that the support exists. Then, use it or let the customer know why your app can't run on their device.

The good news is most of the time, the built-in NativeScript library and several of the plugins will wrap this abstraction for you. So, you do not have to deal with it. However, it is something you would want to keep in mind while writing your application.

Summary

We went through a lot of material here. You learned how to customize your code and screens for any devices using several different types of platform qualifiers. Then, you learned the basics about both the iOS and Android resource systems. You also learned how to add new resources to both platforms. Finally, you got some simple advice to always check for support for anything you need before trying to use it.

In the final chapter, we will see how easy it is to test, debug, and deploy our application.

7
Testing and Deploying Your App

Wow, we are almost done with learning NativeScript. The hard part is behind us. The fun part is about to begin. Testing and debugging! Just so I don't totally ruin your parade, we will discuss a couple of different ways to do testing outside of NativeScript. Then, we will explore how to read the call stack and how to debug your application. Finally, when your application is 100 percent bug free, we will see how to publish it.

In this chapter, we will cover the following topics:

- Testing your application
- Test frameworks
- Local testing of your code
- Unit testing on a device
- Testing on a device
- Understanding the call stack
- Debugging your application
- Publishing your application

Testing your application

Multiple books have been written on testing. There are a dozen ways to build apps using tests and/or test-driven development, and these books cover them well. So, we aren't going to dive into testing as deep as these books do. I personally lean toward doing functional tests and continuous integration testing. However, this subject also requires one complete book.

All we are going to do is cover the basics of how to do tests for your application and the particularities of doing tests with NativeScript. So, without further ado, let's get to it.

Test frameworks

There are several different testing frameworks for JavaScript. So, if you have your own favorite testing framework, most of this advice would also apply to it. In this case, we will use **Mocha**. It is a fairly popular testing framework, so you can easily find many samples and examples on how to use it on the `mochajs.org` website. However, we will get you up and running with NativeScript. The first thing you need to do is open a terminal shell and install `mocha` with the `npm install -g mocha` command. The `-g` option will tell `npm` to install `mocha` globally, just like we did when we installed the `nativescript` command. By making it globally available, you can run it just by typing `mocha` anywhere.

> Mocha is a JavaScript testing framework. This framework runs under node, so everything we are doing with the testing is all using node-based code. This might be confusing sometimes as JavaScript is simpler compared to NativeScript. So, even though we are loading and testing our code that we wrote for NativeScript, it is actually running under node and not NativeScript. This means we have no access to any NativeScript libraries.

Next, you need to navigate to your main project folder and create a new `test` folder. The `test` folder is where you will put all your tests. If you type `mocha` now, it will print **0 passing**, since you have 0 tests. The first example test we will create is a `TestAjaxSocket.js` file inside the `test` folder. It will contain the following lines of code:

```
// Require our AjaxSocket class
var AjaxSocket = require ('../app/AjaxSocket');
```

```
// Require the built in Node assert class
var assert = require('assert');

// Overwrite these functions, as this test unit does not test actual
sending or actual receiving
AjaxSocket.prototype.send = function(s) {
  this._handler("send",
  '{"clientId":1,"messages":[{"from":"me"}]}');
};
AjaxSocket.prototype._handleListener = function() { };

// Create a new AjaxSocket class
var socket  = new AjaxSocket();

// Describe and implement the tests
describe('Ajax Properties', function() {
  describe('#setName', function () {
    it('should = the name we set', function () {
      socket.setName("Awesome");
      assert.equal(socket.getName(), "Awesome");
    });
  });
  describe('#setHost', function () {
    it('should not be null', function () {
      socket.setHost("Book");
      assert.notEqual(socket.getHost(), null);
    });
  });
});

describe('Ajax Send/Receive', function() {
  describe('#Send', function () {
    it('done should be called with a fake packet', function (done)
    {
      socket.on("message", function(d) {
        assert.equal(d.from, 3);
        done();
      });
      socket.send("This is an Awesome Book!");
    });
  });
});
```

In the preceding test, we require our `AjaxSocket` class, which is what we will test, and the built-in node assert library. Next, we will describe two separate tests. One set of tests is to test our two setters. The other test actually will test the receiving code and message handling. You can describe as many tests as you want and group them easily using the `describe` command.

Mocha alone is good to create unit tests of any of our standalone components that don't touch any NativeScript code. So, in this case, to even make it simpler, we created a function that eliminated the need for the Ajax component to actually talk to a server. If you download the source code from the repo, you will see another test file that will actually test communicating with the server. The idea is that this file tests some of the functionality without requiring a server running. We then extend it to test the parts that haven't been tested, including tests for actual server responses. I typically have both offline and online tests so that I can run a group of tests without the server running to verify that, at least, the basics haven't broken while I make any changes. Then, I'll activate a server and run the tests that require a server. This is why this test is designed to test everything without a server.

Now, you might be thinking, "Wait a second! You just wrote that Mocha is good for standalone components that don't touch actual NativeScript code. Isn't this book on NativeScript?" Good catch! Let me explain. When you separate your logic from the NativeScript code, you can easily create unit tests to test using any one of the standard frameworks such as Mocha. However, since the NativeScript code itself currently only runs on the actual devices or device emulators to run any tests that actually use NativeScript code, you need to run the process on a device that supports NativeScript. Your development machine doesn't actually support running pretty much any of the NativeScript common core code. Fortunately, there are ways around this that we will look at before we look at how to test your final application on a device.

Local testing of your code

Let's look at testing the `WebSocketWrapper.js` file. At the top of it, it requires `nativescript-websockets` code. Well, the `nativescript-websockets` code only runs on Android or iOS. It doesn't run on your development machine. So, how are you going to test it?

You will use **Proxyquire**. Proxyquire is a Nifty library that allows you to replace any `require` statements during tests without modifying the code that you are testing. Using it allows you to dynamically replace the functions and classes exported from a module with mock or dummy replacements. A `require` statement would load the exported functions and classes into your code. So, let's look at the top part of the `testWebSockets.js` file:

```
var proxyquire = require('proxyquire');
var assert = require('assert');

var DummyWS = function() {
  this._isOpen = false;
  this._events = {};
};
DummyWS.prototype.on = function(event, callback) {
  if (!this._events[event]) { this._events[event] = [];}
  this._events[event].push(callback);
};
DummyWS.prototype.send = function(m) {
  for (var i=0;i<this._events.message.length;i++) {
    this._events.message[i](this, '{"clientId":1, "from":"SERVER",
    "message":"'+m+'"');
  }
};
DummyWS.prototype.isOpen = function() { return this._isOpen; };
DummyWS.prototype.close = function() { this._isOpen = false; };
DummyWS.prototype.open = function() { this._isOpen = true; };
DummyWS['@noCallThru'] = true;

var WebSocket = proxyquire('../app/WebSocketWrapper',
{"nativescript-websockets": DummyWS});

var socket = new WebSocket();
```

So, what do we have here? First, we require `proxyquire` and `assert`. Proxyquire is going to do our magic for us. We need something to replace `nativescript-websockets` code since that code is incompatible with our developer machine. So, we will create a dummy `WebSocket` class, which will emulate the `nativescript-websocket` class. We have to stub the `constructor`, `on`, `send`, `isOpen`, `close`, and finally, the `open` functions. These are the only `nativescript-websockets` functions we will call from our `WebSocketWrapper` class. We also added `@noCallThru = true` to our class, which is actually a parameter for Proxyquire. This parameter tells Proxyquire to skip attempting to load the real `nativescript-websockets` class.

Normally, Proxyquire will still load the underlying library that was in the `require` statement. Then, you will use Proxyquire to replace a couple of functions. In NativeScript, since the plugins and common code are all Android or ObjectiveC code, they will totally fail to run. That is why we have to configure Proxyquire to skip loading the original library. The next line is where we will use Proxyquire instead of the `require` statement.

To install Proxyquire, you just need to use `npm install --save-dev proxyquire` in your application directory. The `--save-dev` option tells `npm` to install it only as a developer requirement. This will make sure Proxyquire does not get deployed to the app when the `nativescript` command builds your application, as only actual app requirements get built into the application.

Proxyquire takes two parameters. The first parameter is which file to load. The second parameter is an object with the all the stubs. So, now, anytime it sees `require('nativescript-websocket')` inside `WebSocketWrapper`, it will instead use our `DummyWS` class. Pretty sweet, huh? Using Proxyquire, you can stub out any NativeScript code you want. This allows you to test your code as if it were using the real NativeScript library on your local machine. The rest of the code in this file is exactly the same as the `TestAjaxSocket.js` file:

```
describe('WebSockets Properties', function() {
  describe('#setName', function () {
    it('should = the name we set', function () {
      socket.setName("Awesome");
      assert.equal(socket.getName(), "Awesome");
    });
  });
  describe('#setHost', function () {
    it('should not be null', function () {
      socket.setHost("Book");
      assert.notEqual(socket.getHost(), null);
    });
  });
});

describe('WebSocket Send/Receive', function() {
  describe('#Send', function () {
    it('done should be called with a fake packet', function (done)
    {
```

```
        socket.on("message", function(d) {
          assert.equal(d.from, 3);
          done();
        });
        socket.send("This is an Awesome Book!");
      });
    });
  });
```

So now, we have two of the modules from our application tested anytime we run Mocha in the main application folder.

Using Proxyquire, we can even add tests of the `main-page.js` and `settings.js` pages. It would require you to create several dummy wrappers for the NativeScript libraries that are currently being used. You would do it just like we created for the `nativescript-websockets` library. By doing so, it would allow you to actually test your screen's code for any logic issue on your development system.

Unit testing on the device

During the final review of the book, the master branch (the totally unreleased versions) of the `nativescript` command introduced the brand new `nativescript test` command. Fortunately, I saw something appear in the repos and asked about it. Yours truly, living totally dangerously, pulled the absolute latest and greatest master versions of everything so that I can document the all new bleeding-edge way to do unit testing on devices and emulators.

The latest and greatest daily master runtimes are automatically built for all platforms on `http://nativescript.rocks` as a community service. So, in all reality, it was a simple download and install, and then I was running the latest and greatest bleeding-edge NativeScript code. Typically, the only reason you run from master is if you need a fix or some feature that isn't going to show up until the next major release, which might be a while from now.

Until now, we were trying to test our code outside of NativeScript. This is an awesome way to create unit tests that have full access to NativeScript and the device. Your unit tests will actually be running on an emulator or a real device under NativeScript runtimes. This does not discount the ways explained earlier to do unit testing, as these ways run much faster and can be easily off-loaded to an integration server. However, this way can give you a much better picture of the entire project, as it is obviously running your code on the NativeScript platform.

Installing the test framework

You can install the test framework using a simple `nativescript test init` command. It will then ask you which test framework you want to use. At the time of writing this book, it currently has support for Jasmine, Mocha, and QUnit. For the sake of simplicity, I would recommend that you standardize on one framework so that all your tests are written the same way if you choose to do any of the other off-device testing in addition to on-device testing. All three are great test frameworks. To help you understand this chapter, I would recommend that you choose Mocha as we have already used it for the preceding tests, and I will use it for the next test.

It will automatically create a folder called `tests` in the `app` folder. This is where you want to put any tests that you want to run on a device.

Writing tests

If you choose Mocha, the tests are exactly the same as we explored earlier in this chapter. So, let's create a test based on the other tests we have done. Let's take the `websocket` test and actually make it run against our server. The following code will actually test the `websocket` library:

```
var WebSocket = require ("nativescript-websockets");

// We have to open the websocket to our server;
// use the same ip address that we used in crossCommunicator.
// Again on my box it is 192.168.56.1
// Don't forget the server outputs its ip's
var socket = new WebSocket("ws://192.168.56.1:3000");
socket.open();

describe('WebSocket Send/Receive', function() {
  // We generate a random message; to verify we get it back
  var rnd = parseInt(Math.random()*100000,10).toString();

  describe('#Send', function () {
    it('WS message handler should be called with packets',
    function (done) {
      var hasCalledDone = false;
      var counter = 0;
      socket.on("message", function(ws, d) {
        counter++;
        // The first message from the server should be
        // the setClient command
```

```
          if (counter === 1) {
            var hasCommand = d.indexOf
            ("{\"command\":\"setClient\",\"clientId\":");
            assert.equal(hasCommand, 0);
          } else {
            // Wait for our message back
            if (d === '{"from":"ME","message":"'+rnd+'"}') {
              if (!hasCalledDone) {
                hasCalledDone = true;
                done();
              }
            }
          }
        });
        socket.send(JSON.stringify({from: "TEST", message: rnd}));
      });
    });
  });
```

The preceding test basically opens websocket, creates a random message, and sends it. The message listener then listens for messages. The first message should always be the `setClient` message from the server. The following messages are all messages that the server has queued up to send to new users. Finally, it will send back the message you sent with your random message. We will compare this, and if we find it, then we will run the `done()` command, which tells Mocha that this test was successful. Otherwise, the test will timeout and show up as a failure. Remember that before you run the test, you must start the `crossCommunicator` server. Otherwise, this test won't be able to connect and will fail.

Running tests

Running tests is equally easy. All you have to do is type `tns test android` or `tns test ios` to start the test process. This launches the process on your local machine and then copies the test and all the NativeScript code to your device. With the current beta version of the command, I ran into an issue where it wouldn't automatically launch the test application. Once it finally stated it had successfully deployed the application, I just had to manually launch the app on the device. Otherwise, it actually ran and performed all the tests and then automatically quit out of everything. Your terminal windows where you ran `tns test` will show you the status of all the tests. The Telerik team should be proud. They did a great job of integrating multiple pieces and making a nice working unit test system for NativeScript.

Testing your app on a device or emulator

Now that we looked at how to do different types of unit testing on your local machine and on the device, the next step is to actually have tests that run your actual app on an emulator or device. Nothing can beat an actual test of your full application on the device that you are using and targeting. The more automated the testing is, the easier it is for you to detect issues in your code while you are developing and enhancing your application.

There is an open source project called **Appium** that we will use. It is located at `http://appium.io`. This project supports iOS and Android, which makes it a perfect fit to do all of our on-device testing. To install it globally, you need to use `npm install -g appium` command. Then, in your main project folder, you need to also use `npm install --save-dev wd`, which will install the JavaScript driver that you can use to drive your application from your developer machine in JavaScript. We will continue to use Mocha to run our tests and report any issues.

Appium has many demos available to help you build complete application test coverage. Some fairly good documentation to walk you through things is at `http://appium.io/slate/en/v1.1.0`, and a large number of examples are at `https://github.com/appium/sample-code`.

The example we will write is going to be for the Android platform. However, in the comments, I will list some slight changes to make it run for iOS. Appium is totally cross platform. However, the underlying native platform UI controls that NativeScript abstracts are not named the same way since they actually call the native iOS and Android controls. Currently, you have to write slightly different tests for each platform.

Before you actually run Mocha on this test, you need to make sure you start the Appium server, open up a new terminal shell, and start Appium by typing `appium` in the terminal shell. So, let's start our journey and create a new `testAppium.js` file:

```
var wd = require('wd');

describe("Appium", function () {
  this.timeout(100000);
  var driver;

  before("Appium Setup", function () {
    driver = wd.promiseChainRemote('localhost', 4723);

    var testFramework = {
      browserName: '',
      'appium-version': '1.3',
      platformName: 'Android', // 'iOS'
```

```
        platformVersion: '4.4',   // '8.1'
        deviceName: '',   // 'iPhone Simulator'
        app: __dirname +
        '/../platforms/android/build/outputs/apk/crossCommunicator-
        debug.apk'
        // __dirname +
        '/../platforms/ios/build/emulator/crossCommunicator.app'
      };

      return driver.init(testFramework).
      setImplicitWaitTimeout(3000);
    });

    after("Appium Setup", function () { return driver.quit(); });

    it("should type in an element", function (done) {
      driver
      .elementByXPath
      ('//android.widget.EditText[@text=\'Enter your name\']')   //
      '//UITextField[@id=\'name\']'
      .sendKeys('Testing')
      .text()
      .then(function (v) {
        if ('Testing' !== v) {
          done(new Error("Value in name field does not match"));
        } else {
          done();
        }
      }, done);
    });
  });
```

We start the test by requiring the `wd` driver. This is the driver that allows us to talk to Appium from your test in JavaScript. The `describe` and `it` functions are just like before, as they are part of Mocha. We now added a couple of new Mocha functions, `before` and `after`. The `before` function is run before any tests; likewise, `after` is run after all the tests. In our `before` function code, we connect to our Appium server. In the `after` function, we disconnect properly from the Appium server to make sure everything is cleaned up. The actual test looks for an element on the screen via the Appium XPath system to see whether they can exist. In our case, the element exists. So, we will send text to the control, followed by checking the controls to verify that it has our new text. It is a rather simple test, but as you can see, we can check in chain with the `find`, `set`, and `get` functions. You can easily set, get, click and check multiple fields per test.

So now, the next time you run `mocha`, it will actually test that the settings screen name field works on the emulator along with the `WebSocket` and `AjaxSocket` tests.

Understanding the call stack

We will switch tracks. The other side of the equation is debugging your application when it breaks. Nobody is perfect at coding, so understanding the call stack is an important factor in figuring out why your application has just crashed. Both Android and iOS report the call stack slightly differently. So, we shall examine Android first and then finish up with iOS call stack. So, open up your `main-page.js` file, and on line three, add the bogus code: `Stock.blah();`.

Android call stack

On Android, you get the call stack in two different places. When the application crashes, it normally creates a log in the actual application that you can view and it looks like this:

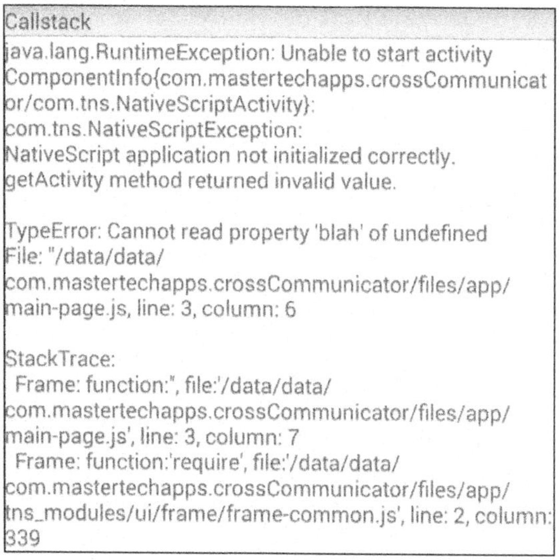

```
Callstack
java.lang.RuntimeException: Unable to start activity
ComponentInfo{com.mastertechapps.crossCommunicat
or/com.tns.NativeScriptActivity}:
com.tns.NativeScriptException:
NativeScript application not initialized correctly.
getActivity method returned invalid value.

TypeError: Cannot read property 'blah' of undefined
File: "/data/data/
com.mastertechapps.crossCommunicator/files/app/
main-page.js, line: 3, column: 6

StackTrace:
 Frame: function:'', file:'/data/data/
com.mastertechapps.crossCommunicator/files/app/
main-page.js', line: 3, column: 7
 Frame: function:'require', file:'/data/data/
com.mastertechapps.crossCommunicator/files/app/
tns_modules/ui/frame/frame-common.js', line: 2, column:
339
```

As you can see, about half way down on the screen, in the error report, there is the actual error. The error is **TypeError: cannot read property 'blah' of undefined**. In this case, I put it on line 3, column 6. In this case, the error actually points to the issue directly. Sometimes, you get lucky, and the error actually is straightforward. So, you look at line 3, around character 6 of the `main-page.js` file, and you would see that we put `Stock.blah();` as the code. This, of course, is totally broken since `Stock` hasn't been defined, and so `blah` is not even a function of `Stock`. If you look at the screen closely, you would see `StackTrace:` and then the file, line, and column of each function that was called to get to this point of where it failed. Most of the time, you can use the `StackTrace` as shown in your app when it crashes. However, there are a couple of cases where you won't get an in-app stack trace.

The second place you can see the stack trace is in the terminal where you started the app from the application logging. So, you would see something like this:

```
node-gyp
I/ActivityManager(  522): Start proc com.mastertechapps.crossCommunicator for activity com.mastertec
happs.crossCommunicator/com.tns.NativeScriptActivity: pid=1695 uid=10066 gids={50066, 1028, 1015, 30
03}
D/dalvikvm( 1695): Late-enabling CheckJNI
D/dalvikvm( 1695): Trying to load lib /data/app-lib/com.mastertechapps.crossCommunicator-1/libAssetE
xtractor.so 0xa5094ae8
D/dalvikvm( 1695): Added shared lib /data/app-lib/com.mastertechapps.crossCommunicator-1/libAssetExt
ractor.so 0xa5094ae8
D/dalvikvm( 1695): No JNI_OnLoad found in /data/app-lib/com.mastertechapps.crossCommunicator-1/libAs
setExtractor.so 0xa5094ae8, skipping init
D/dalvikvm( 1695): Trying to load lib /data/app-lib/com.mastertechapps.crossCommunicator-1/libNative
Script.so 0xa5094ae8
D/dalvikvm( 1695): Added shared lib /data/app-lib/com.mastertechapps.crossCommunicator-1/libNativeSc
ript.so 0xa5094ae8
I/TNS.Native( 1695): NativeScript Runtime Version 1.3.0, commit 0fe4dfa732bef9cdd745c4e025913a1a618b
3383
D/TNS.Native( 1695): JNI_ONLoad
D/TNS.Native( 1695): JNI_ONLoad END
D/TNS.Native( 1695): lenNodes=58800, lenNames=601913, lenValues=669165
D/TNS.Native( 1695): time=1
D/TNS.Java( 1695): port=-1
D/dalvikvm( 1695): GC_CONCURRENT freed 294K, 12% free 3617K/4072K, paused 1ms+1ms, total 3ms
D/dalvikvm( 1695): GC_CONCURRENT freed 319K, 12% free 3701K/4180K, paused 0ms+0ms, total 2ms
D/dalvikvm( 1695): GC_CONCURRENT freed 312K, 11% free 3863K/4336K, paused 1ms+2ms, total 4ms
D/dalvikvm( 1695): GC_CONCURRENT freed 569K, 17% free 3714K/4444K, paused 0ms+1ms, total 2ms
D/dalvikvm( 1695): GC_CONCURRENT freed 378K, 16% free 3772K/4444K, paused 0ms+0ms, total 2ms
E/TNS.Native( 1695): TypeError: Cannot read property 'blah' of undefined
E/TNS.Native( 1695): File: "/data/data/com.mastertechapps.crossCommunicator/files/app/main-page.js,
line: 3, column: 6
E/TNS.Native( 1695): StackTrace:
E/TNS.Native( 1695):     Frame: function:'', file:'/data/data/com.mastertechapps.crossCommunicator/fi
les/app/main-page.js', line: 3, column: 7
E/TNS.Native( 1695):     Frame: function:'require', file:'/data/data/com.mastertechapps.crossCommunic
ator/files/app/tns_modules/ui/frame/frame-common.js', line: 2, column: 339
E/TNS.Native( 1695):     Frame: function:'resolvePageFromEntry', file:'/data/data/com.mastertechapps.
crossCommunicator/files/app/tns_modules/ui/frame/frame-common.js', line: 45, column: 29
E/TNS.Native( 1695):     Frame: function:'Frame.navigate', file:'/data/data/com.mastertechapps.crossC
ommunicator/files/app/tns_modules/ui/frame/frame-common.js', line: 110, column: 20
E/TNS.Native( 1695):     Frame: function:'AndroidApplication.getActivity', file:'/data/data/com.maste
rtechapps.crossCommunicator/files/app/tns_modules/application/application.js', line: 140, column: 26

E/TNS.Native( 1695):     Frame: function:'app.init.getActivity', file:'/data/data/com.mastertechapps.
crossCommunicator/files/app/tns_modules/application/application.js', line: 111, column: 32
E/TNS.Native( 1695): TypeError: Cannot read property 'blah' of undefined
E/TNS.Native( 1695): File: "/data/data/com.mastertechapps.crossCommunicator/files/app/main-page.js,
line: 3, column: 6
E/TNS.Native( 1695): StackTrace:
E/TNS.Native( 1695):     Frame: function:'', file:'/data/data/com.mastertechapps.crossCommunicator/fi
les/app/main-page.js', line: 3, column: 7
E/TNS.Native( 1695):     Frame: function:'require', file:'/data/data/com.mastertechapps.crossCommunic
ator/files/app/tns_modules/ui/frame/frame-common.js', line: 2, column: 339
```

As you can see, about half way down the screen is the same **TypeError: Cannot read property 'blah' of undefined** error. It also lists the same `StackTrace` code. Now, one word of caution: I have seen where the in-app error `StackTrace` code was wrong, and the `StackTrace` code at the terminal was correct. So, if the StackTrace you are looking at in the application doesn't make any sense, double-check the terminal and see whether it has a better `StackTrace`. For the majority of the time, the stack traces will match, so just look at the application stack track as it is easier to read without all the additional logging.

iOS call stack

On the iOS platform, the call stack is on the terminal as well. However, the majority of the stack trace is the actual native runtime and utterly useless. Above the first compiled stack trace line, **1   0xb74c0 NativeScript::FFICallback<NativeScript::ObjCMethodCallback> ::ffiClosureCallback(ffi_cif*, void*, void**, void*)**, you should see something like this line: **file:///app/main-page.js:3:6: JS ERROR ReferenceError: Can't find variable: Stock**. This tells you that the error was in the `main-page.js` file, on line 3, character 6. It looks like this:

```
ulator.sdk/System/Library/Frameworks/CoreGraphics.framework
NativeScript loaded bundle file:///Applications/Xcode.app/Contents/Developer/Platforms/iPhoneSimulator.platform/Developer/SDKs/iPhoneSim
ulator.sdk/System/Library/Frameworks/CoreText.framework
file:///app/main-page.js:3:6: JS ERROR ReferenceError: Can't find variable: Stock
1   0xb74c0 NativeScript::FFICallback<NativeScript::ObjCMethodCallback>::ffiClosureCallback(ffi_cif*, void*, void**, void*)
2   0x693646 ffi_closure_SYSV_inner
3   0x693092 .LCFI7
4   0x14eff24 -[UIViewController loadViewIfRequired]
5   0x14f0215 -[UIViewController view]
6   0x13e7215 -[UIWindow addRootViewControllerViewIfPossible]
7   0x13e7689 -[UIWindow _setHidden:forced:]
8   0x13e7940 -[UIWindow _orderFrontWithoutMakingKey]
9   0x13f5c7d -[UIWindow makeKeyAndVisible]
10  0x692fad .LCFI1
11  0x69358f ffi_call
12  0xb5da1 NativeScript::ObjCMethodCall::derivedExecuteCall(JSC::ExecState*, unsigned char*)
13  0xb6098 long long NativeScript::FFICall::executeCall<NativeScript::ObjCMethodCall>(JSC::ExecState*)
14  0x43a65e JSC::LLInt::setUpCall(JSC::ExecState*, JSC::Instruction*, JSC::CodeSpecializationKind, JSC::JSValue, JSC::LLIntCallLinkInfo
*)
15  0x436b46 llint_slow_path_call
16  0x43f343 llint_entry
17  0x43af06 vmEntryToJavaScript
18  0x3d180c JSC::JITCode::execute(JSC::VM*, JSC::ProtoCallFrame*)
19  0x3b3045 JSC::Interpreter::executeCall(JSC::ExecState*, JSC::JSObject*, JSC::CallType, JSC::CallData const&, JSC::JSValue, JSC::ArgL
ist const&)
20  0x51b97d JSC::call(JSC::ExecState*, JSC::JSValue, JSC::CallType, JSC::CallData const&, JSC::JSValue, JSC::ArgList const&)
21  0x5656dc JSC::boundFunctionCall(JSC::ExecState*)
22  0x7050981d
23  0x43f353 llint_entry
24  0x43af06 vmEntryToJavaScript
25  0x3d180c JSC::JITCode::execute(JSC::VM*, JSC::ProtoCallFrame*)
26  0x3b3045 JSC::Interpreter::executeCall(JSC::ExecState*, JSC::JSObject*, JSC::CallType, JSC::CallData const&, JSC::JSValue, JSC::ArgL
ist const&)
27  0x51b97d JSC::call(JSC::ExecState*, JSC::JSValue, JSC::CallType, JSC::CallData const&, JSC::JSValue, JSC::ArgList const&)
28  0xb73ab NativeScript::FFICallback<NativeScript::ObjCMethodCallback>::callFunction(JSC::JSValue const&, JSC::ArgList const&, void*)
29  0xb673e NativeScript::ObjCMethodCallback::ffiClosureCallback(void*, void**, void*)
30  0xb7484 NativeScript::FFICallback<NativeScript::ObjCMethodCallback>::ffiClosureCallback(ffi_cif*, void*, void**, void*)
31  0x693646 ffi_closure_SYSV_inner
Session ended without errors.
```

Since the JavaScript engine that runs on iOS is different from Android, the error is a bit more precise than Android. On Android, you get **property 'blah' of undefined**, whereas on iOS, you actually get the variable name that is undefined. So sometimes, if the error is confusing on one platform, you can run it on the other platform, and you might be able to get a better picture of the problem.

Debugging your application

NativeScript uses the built-in Chrome debugging tools to allow you to debug your application on Android and a similar set of tools in Safari for iOS. You can start the debugging in one of two ways. You can start the debugging when you launch your application using `nativescript debug android --debug-brk [--device / --emulator / --geny]` to launch your application with the debugger active. The second way is if your application is currently running, you can use `nativescript debug ios --start [ --device / --emulator / --geny]` to connect to an already running application.

NativeScript currently requires a working Internet connection for debugging. It also requires Chrome to be installed to debug Android applications.

Once you have launched the debug tools, you should see something like this on Android:

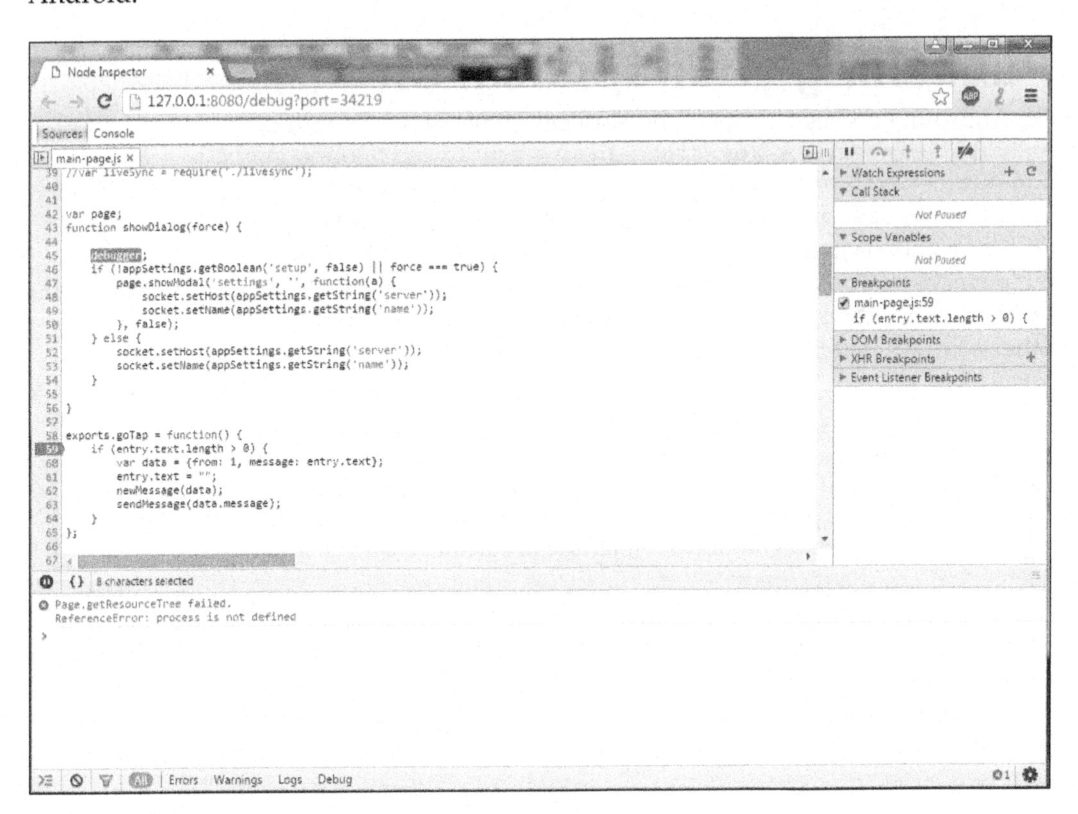

This is the Node inspector that you can use in Chrome to debug your web pages and even node apps. NativeScript is leveraging the same code that Google wrote for Chrome to work in NativeScript. The Developer tools are very powerful and allow you a lot of flexibility. You can easily step through each line of your code or run to the next break point. You can easily add break points in either the code manually using the `debugger;` (see line 45) command or by clicking on the line number (see line 59).

> The `debugger;` command is pretty global through JavaScript. Browsers, node, and even NativeScript can all use it. It causes a debugger to break and stop at that instruction if a debugger is attached. Otherwise, it is ignored.

The iOS interface is similar and also allows you the same abilities to debug your running code. The main thing you need to know is how to start the debugger. Then, it is fairly simple to step through all your code and figure out what is broke.

Publishing your application

On Android, you need to build the application using `nativescript build android --release --key-store-path=<yourfile> --key-store-password=<your password> --key-store-alias=<alias> --key-store-alias-password=<password>`. This will build you a release version of your APK. The APK's location is going to be in your `applications/platforms/Android/build/outputs/APKs`. Make sure you do not take your `debug` package, as it will be rejected by all the app stores. You need a key to sign your application so that Google (and others) knows that this application is from you and only from you.

> To create a keystore, you can use the `keytool` program that comes with the Android SDK. The `keytool` program allows you to create, edit, and delete keys inside the store file. However, there is a cross-platform open source project at `http://keystore-explorer.sourceforge.net/`, which is a graphic user interface to edit and create your keystore.

Once you have built your application to publish your Android application on Google Play Store, you need to have a Google Play account. The main URL to deal with Google Play Store is `https://play.google.com/apps/publish`. Once you have an account, you can easily upload your APK file to it. Another popular location to publish Android apps is the Amazon store at `https://developer.amazon.com/welcome.html`.

Publishing to iOS

On iOS, it is a slightly different process. The first step is to run `tns build ios --release` from the terminal. This will make sure your application is totally up to date. Then, you can follow the instructions that Apple detail at `https://developer.apple.com/library/ios/documentation/IDEs/Conceptual/AppDistributionGuide/SubmittingYourApp/SubmittingYourApp.html`. The main XCode project, as we discussed earlier, is located in the `/platforms/ios/` folder that you will need to open via XCode to submit to the Apple iOS Store.

> If you are using any plugins that use **cocoapods**, then the main project file is actually named with `projectname.xcworkspace` rather than with `projectname.xcodeproj`. So, when you open this up in Xcode to submit the application, make sure you open the `projectname.xcworkspace` project.

Summary

We covered a lot on debugging and testing in this chapter. You learned several techniques on how to test your application. You learned how to build and run tests on your development box and on emulators or real devices. Appium is really awesome if you spend time to build coverage of all your code. For the most part, the tests are fairly cross platform with minor changes to the field types.

In addition, we covered how to actually debug your application, which can be very important when attempting to figure out why something isn't working as expected.

If you are looking for a specific file or what it does, remember to check out all the locations listed in *Chapter 2, The Project Structure*. This chapter can help greatly when you are trying to figure out where to stick something in a new project.

When you are in need of a cool feature, don't forget to check out all the cool plugins and the sites where you can find them. It is normally better to reuse other tested code than to build your own. Third-party components are real life savers for being able to quickly develop a new application.

As a last bit of advice, we covered a lot of information in *Chapter 6, Platform Differences*, including platform differences and different screen resolutions. This is critical information to build a good looking cross-platform application. You have to worry about devices in multiple eco systems, so try and take into account all the similarities you can between your targets. Then, you need to use the platform specifics to build out your customizations for each platform.

Now, you have the tools you need installed and, most importantly, you now know how to build a cross-platform application and test and debug it. Finally, you now know how to become a billionaire by submitting your awesome application to all the major stores.

Index

Symbols

A

B

C

D

E

F

G

H

I

K

L

M

N

P

R

S

T

U

V

W

X

Thank you for buying
Getting Started with NativeScript

About Packt Publishing

Packt, pronounced 'packed', published its first book, *Mastering phpMyAdmin for Effective MySQL Management*, in April 2004, and subsequently continued to specialize in publishing highly focused books on specific technologies and solutions.

Our books and publications share the experiences of your fellow IT professionals in adapting and customizing today's systems, applications, and frameworks. Our solution-based books give you the knowledge and power to customize the software and technologies you're using to get the job done. Packt books are more specific and less general than the IT books you have seen in the past. Our unique business model allows us to bring you more focused information, giving you more of what you need to know, and less of what you don't.

Packt is a modern yet unique publishing company that focuses on producing quality, cutting-edge books for communities of developers, administrators, and newbies alike. For more information, please visit our website at `www.packtpub.com`.

About Packt Open Source

In 2010, Packt launched two new brands, Packt Open Source and Packt Enterprise, in order to continue its focus on specialization. This book is part of the Packt Open Source brand, home to books published on software built around open source licenses, and offering information to anybody from advanced developers to budding web designers. The Open Source brand also runs Packt's Open Source Royalty Scheme, by which Packt gives a royalty to each open source project about whose software a book is sold.

Writing for Packt

We welcome all inquiries from people who are interested in authoring. Book proposals should be sent to `author@packtpub.com`. If your book idea is still at an early stage and you would like to discuss it first before writing a formal book proposal, then please contact us; one of our commissioning editors will get in touch with you.

We're not just looking for published authors; if you have strong technical skills but no writing experience, our experienced editors can help you develop a writing career, or simply get some additional reward for your expertise.

Learning TypeScript

ISBN: 978-1-78398-554-8 Paperback: 368 pages

Exploit the features of TypeScript to develop and maintain captivating web applications with ease

1. Learn how to develop modular, scalable, maintainable, and adaptable web applications by taking advantage of TypeScript.
2. Create object-oriented JavaScript that adheres to the solid principles efficiently.
3. A comprehensive guide that explains the fundamentals of TypeScript with the help of practical examples.

Mastering TypeScript

ISBN: 978-1-78439-966-5 Paperback: 364 pages

Build enterprise-ready, industrial strength web applications using TypeScript and leading JavaScript frameworks

1. Focus on test-driven development to help build quality applications that are modular, scalable, maintainable, and adaptable.
2. Practical examples that show you how to use TypeScript with popular JavaScript frameworks including Backbone, Angular, Node.js, require.js, and Marionette.
3. Enhance your TypeScript knowledge with in-depth discussions on language features, third-party libraries, declaration files, and so on using practical scenarios.

Please check **www.PacktPub.com** for information on our titles

CPSIA information can be obtained
at www.ICGtesting.com
Printed in the USA
BVOW09s1109251116
468829BV00010B/149/P